The
GREATER
CLEVELAND
GARDEN
GUIDE

Susan McClure

The

GREATER
CLEVELAND
GARDEN
GUIDE

Susan McClure

GRAY & COMPANY, PUBLISHERS

CLEVELAND

Acknowledgements

Thanks to the scores of Cleveland area gardeners who make northeast Ohio so rich horticulturally—they provide the resources for this resource guide. And thanks to Alex Apanius and the staff of The Garden Center, Eliot Paine and the staff of Holden Arboretum, Jack Kerrigan of the Cooperative Extension Service, Richard Kay of Breezewood Gardens, and Barbara Gray for reviewing the manuscript. Thanks also to my husband, Ted, who cooked some excellent dinners while I worked to finish this project!

GRAY & COMPANY, PUBLISHERS
11000 CEDAR AVENUE
CLEVELAND, OHIO 44106

Library of Congress Cataloging-in-Publication Data
McClure, Susan, 1957–
The Greater Cleveland garden guide / Susan McClure.
1. Gardening—Ohio—Cleveland Region. 2. Gardening—Ohio—Cleveland Region—Directories. 3. Gardens—Ohio—Cleveland Region—Guidebooks. 4. Horticulture—Ohio—Cleveland Region—Directories. 5. Gardening—Study and teaching—Ohio—Cleveland Region—Directories. 6. Gardening—Ohio—Cleveland Region—Societies, etc. 7. Natural Resources—Ohio—Cleveland Region. I. Title.

SB453.2.03M38 1993
635.9´09771´32-DC20   93-7265

ISBN 0-9631738-3-9

FIRST PRINTING
Printed in the United States of America

10 9 8 7 6 5 4 3 2 1

Contents

Introduction

HAVE YOU EVER NEEDED A SOLUTION to a particular gardening problem but not known where to look? When you need help with a complicated task, such as pruning, tackling pests, or landscaping, do you know how to choose the right professional for the job? Do you sometimes think about taking classes in gardening or botany—or even toy with the idea of beginning a career in horticulture? Are you interested in meeting people with similar gardening interests to trade information and share secrets? Would you like to know more about the gardens in this area that you can tour for recreation and inspiration?

If any of the above apply to you, like most gardeners in this area you probably know that the answers you need exist. But they are sometimes hard to find.

Do you sometimes wonder why a friend has sandy soil while you have clay—and what you can do about it? Do Cleveland's droughts and downpours cause problems for your landscape and headaches for you? Have you ever wanted to make your garden or landscape more successful with less work? Does your garden ever get behind schedule because a few tasks have slipped your mind?

There are solutions to these problems, too, if you know whom to ask, where to look, and what too look for.

The greater Cleveland area has a wonderfully rich and diverse population of gardens and gardeners and a resulting wide range of gardening resources. This book is meant to bring together in a single handy guide the best and most useful of these many resources and to tell where, when, and how

to find out more about them. In it are the answers to these questions and many more like them. It will help you:

- Navigate the vast network of gardening professionals and suppliers.
- Understand climate and soil and how they affect your garden and landscapes.
- Plan a calendar of necessary tasks for every month of the year.
- Get help for common problems and guidance for evaluating your landscape and making landscape improvements.
- Discover special gardens to tour.
- Learn about programs to further your garden education.
- Gain access to horticultural groups and plant societies.
- Find where to turn for more information.

This book is designed to open doors for all gardeners—easily, accurately, sensibly.

Using This Book

Plant Names

Whenever possible, I have called plants by their common names—for example, rose and daylily. On occasion, however, I must refer to the more specific botanical name in order to avoid confusion with other plants. Even if you don't care to use these botanical names when you are talking with friends, they can be useful when you want to order plants or review information on them in other texts.

A botanical name consists of genus and species, which are written in italics. The genus name is always capitalized. For instance, rose in the genus *Rosa*. The species name is not capitalized, as with the old-fashioned species of fragrant French rose, *Rosa gallica.*

Often you also will find a variety name (indicating an improvement or variation on a species that has occurred naturally and been propagated for gardens) or cultivar name (indicating a plant that is known only in cultivation and was hybridized in a breeding program, cloned, or developed from a man-made mutation). Variety names are written in italics. Cultivars are capitalized and enclosed in apostrophes. For instance the creeping blue-green-leaved sargent juniper is *Juniperus chinensis* 'Glauca'. Although this cultivar may grow like other creeping junipers, 'Glauca' differs because it holds its blue-green color especially well in winter. If you like that look, look for this cultivar name on a nursery tag or in a catalog. Likewise, you can find cultivars with special characteristics for nearly every type of landscape or garden plant—just look for a cultivar name and explanation of the cultivar's special characteristics. (You may have to ask salespeople or check reference books to find out how a cultivar differs from the species and from other cultivars.)

Hybrid plants, the result of interbreeding two or more species, will be indicated by an "x" placed between the generic name and the species name. For instance, the old-fashioned alba rose is written *Rosa* x *alba.* This hybrid is also available in cultivars such as *Rosa* x *alba* 'Incarnata', which has white blooms tinged in pink.

Occasionally, when hybrid plants have many parents, we may leave out the species name and refer to the plant by genus and cultivar. One example is the Meidiland roses, new disease-resistant, extra hardy, hybrid shrub roses from France. The botanical name for a scarlet-flowered type with arching three-foot-long fronds is *Rosa* 'Scarlet Meidiland'. Occasionally, when cultivars come from overseas, you may also see the original, foreign name listed. For 'Scarlet Meidiland', the French cultivar name is 'Meikrotal' P.P. 6087.

You can find most species names listed in *Hortus Third* (1976, MacMillan, New York, NY), a massive dictionary of cultivated plants. For more information on the process and meaning of botanical nomenclature, look for the classic book *Botanical Latin* (by William Stern, 3rd Ed. 1983, David and Charles Publishing, North Pomfret, VT), or *Gardener's Latin* (by Bill Neal, 1992, Algonquin Books, Chapel Hill, NC), a fun, small book that will tell you what some of these botanical names mean.

Horticultural Terms

I may occasionally use horticultural terms that are not familiar to you. Some of these may prove valuable—for example, by helping you clearly explain a process or problem when talking to a landscaper or experienced gardener. Horticultural terms that may be uncommon are accompanied by a brief description.

References

Cross-references within the text indicate related entries in other sections and chapters.

You may want further information or details about some subjects discussed in this book. When an especially good book exists, I have referred you to it. Most of these can be obtained from local bookstores or libraries. There is also a list of some publishers that specialize in gardening books and a guide to area gardening libraries in chapter 2.

Data

Please note that addresses, dates, times, and other data were accurate when collected but are always subject to change.

The
GREATER
CLEVELAND
GARDEN
GUIDE

CHAPTER ONE

Gardens to View and Appreciate

LIKE HOME-DECORATING ENTHUSIASTS who tour beautiful homes or attend real estate open houses just to see what fabulous places really look like inside, people who garden like to see what other people are doing with *their* gardens. Fortunately for us, northeast Ohio boasts a great number and wide variety of public and semipublic gardens. This chapter introduces many of this area's best gardens, particularly those in which you can enjoy the sights and also learn a few things that will help you with your own garden.

For example, if you are curious about how to keep weeds down in perennial beds, each of twenty perennial gardens listed here may have a unique way to tackle weeds. If you are thinking about adding an Oriental influence to your landscape, sample the Japanese gardens at The Garden Center of Greater Cleveland and Stan Hywet Hall. If you love the fragrance of flowering lilacs or crab apples or enjoy the sight of big sweeps of spring bulbs, immerse yourself in them at the Cleveland Museum of Art, Falconskeape Gardens, and Lake View Cemetery. For different perspectives on English gardening, try Gardenview Horticultural Park and Claystone. Still other gardens will give you ideas for different ways to grow indoor plants, herbs, wildflowers, edibles, roses, and trees.

There are hundreds of wonderful home landscapes and gardens in northeast Ohio that are fun to pass by and ogle from the street or, better yet, tour with a plant society or during a community fund raiser. (To find out more about garden tours, see Home and Garden Tours in chapter 2.) The gardens listed here are generally open to the public during certain hours and months, though a few will open their gates only by advance appointment.

The gardens range in scale from modest to grandiose and feature many different themes, types of plants, and garden layouts. Each has particular strengths. Some shine in spring or peak in fall; others change focus throughout the seasons.

I have divided the garden areas into those where you can drop in unannounced and those where you will need advance appointments. They are listed in alphabetical order by garden name. For more details about the organizations behind the gardens, associated educational activities, or attached nursery areas, follow the cross-references to other chapters.

Gardens Open to the Public

Brecksville Nature Center, Metroparks
(Brecksville Reservation, Chippewa Creek Drive, Brecksville; 526-1012)

Behind a spring wildflower garden you will find a unique two-acre prairie area. It's not a true garden but a re-created ecosystem (a system of interacting living things and nonliving environment) similar to that which grew in this area centuries ago when weather conditions were drier. You can observe the prairie close-up from a walking path that cuts through it or scan it from the observation deck above. In late summer, this prairie is spectacular with its towering grasses and flowers, and since prairie wildflowers such as coneflower and blazing-star have an important place in gardens, you might see something here that will give you ideas for home.

Naturalist Karl Smith and his staff collected seeds for all the plants here from within Ohio (even though similar seeds can be bought from nurseries in prairie states to the west). They are adamant about keeping the prairie a pure-as-possible replica of local history. Smith has included Ohio species of goldenrod, lilies, lady's-slipper orchids, mountain mint, spiderwort, violets, giant sunflowers, boneset, butterfly weed, and cordgrass.

"Unlike a garden, we make no attempt to control the animals—they have free interaction. So the area is heavily browsed by deer, groundhogs, rabbits. Voles, at one point, cut all the stems off at ground level. Caterpillars eat the greenery, then turn into butterflies that visit the flowers. But we do attempt to control the plants, to maintain the area as a prairie." Smith keeps woody trees and shrubs from invading the Brecksville Reservation prairie by burning it annually.

Cahoon Memorial Rose Garden
(Cahoon Memorial Park, Cahoon and Lake roads, Bay Village)

This charming collection of roses is situated in Bay Village's Cahoon Park, within sight of Lake Erie. A white picket fence encloses a traditional garden; inside, a thousand rose-bushes throw out lots of bright color, even in the rain. On the perimeter of the garden, roses ramble up along the fence; inside, the beds form circles surrounding a central sundial memorial.

"This is a traditional design, used by the Incas and other cultures because it has a pattern similar to the sun. There is a central circle and paths that radiate out from it like the rays of the sun. The other curving beds complement the central circle, which in this case is a memorial to World War II, Korean and Vietnam War veterans," said Frank Aleksandrowicz, the garden's volunteer designer who cared for the rose garden for eight years. In addition to the circular layout, a triangular bed surrounds the bulky base of the flagpole and lateral strips of roses run east to west at the south end of the garden.

Cahoon Memorial Rose Garden is an American Rose Society display garden, so it always has some of the best new varieties on display. Debbie Sutherland, curator, said this garden houses over a hundred different varieties of miniatures, hybrid teas, floribundas, grandifloras, shrub roses, and old garden roses—in short, almost anything a rose grower could want to see.

"When I was planning the garden," said designer Aleksandrowicz, "I tried to find historic English rose types that were repeat bloomers [most historic roses bloom only once in spring] so that the whole garden keeps flowering all summer. It seems to me that this is important for a public rose garden. You want people to come back in June, July, August, and September and say each time, 'Hey, this is nice', because there is so much happening."

"When all the roses bloom, their scent is so wonderful—it out-smells anything else around," said Sutherland. "People just love the place, but for different reasons. One woman comes out to photograph monarch butterflies only on cloudy days. Another person videotapes the garden and puts it to music. Some people come up to get ideas for their own garden. A lot of folks stopped by in 1992 to see if we were having as much trouble with black spot [a fungus disease of roses] as they were at home. One man came by specifically to see 'Dolly Parton', a very temperamental hybrid tea rose, which I sprayed weekly and still couldn't keep clean."

Cleveland Metroparks
(for a directory and map describing the Metroparks, call 351-6300)

The park system circling greater Cleveland is primarily a place for natural scenery and recreation, but it also includes a few gardens well worth visiting. Herb and wildflower gardens cluster near several nature centers, combining the outdoors with facilities for discovering more about plants and how people and animals interact with them. The following Metroparks facilities are described elsewhere within this section's alphabetical listing:

- Brecksville Nature Center
- Cleveland Metroparks Zoo
- Cleveland Metroparks Zoo RainForest
- Garfield Park Nature Center
- Rocky River Nature Center
- Sanctuary Marsh Nature Center

Cleveland Metroparks Zoo
(3900 Brookside Park Dr., Cleveland, 44109; 661-6500; admission fee; discount for members of the Cleveland Zoological Society)

Like many zoological parks nationwide, the Cleveland Zoo has expanded its horticultural exhibits, which now include over two thousand plant species and make the zoo a prettier place to visit and a more comfortable home for the animals. The zoo staff also plans to label the plants in most areas over the next couple of years. "Recently I've been hearing visitors comparing our landscaping to other zoos, which shows people are noticing what we are doing," said Don Krock, assistant park manager in charge of horticulture and service maintenance.

Take a moment as you walk through the zoo to look at the display gardens situated at strategic locations around the park.

Specialty gardens highlight conifers, ornamental grasses, and annual and perennial plants. An alpine rock garden occupies a slope near the seal and polar bear corner of the zoo. Krock is experimenting with new hardy plants from Australia and New Zealand around the Outback Railroad area, where kids like to go to see kangaroos boxing. Although the small display greenhouse overlooking the giraffe yard is often overlooked, you should stop in there to find wonderful cacti, tropicals, orchids, and seasonal flowers. An animal flower garden outside the greenhouse is devoted entirely to plants with animal-related names like tiger marigold and hen-and-chickens.

Other gardens depict the flora of an animal's homeland. One such garden surrounds the three-quarter-acre outdoor gorilla enclosure. Inside the enclosure, landscaping simulates a gorilla's natural habitat with tropical forest-type plants—bamboos, grasses, and trees (hot-wired to keep gorillas from climbing them). To give visitors an even better feeling for the wild areas where gorillas play, the walkway nearby is heavily landscaped to simulate a tropical rain forest. Of course this isn't the tropics, so Krock has substituted plants that he hopes will be hardy, including:

- Big-leaved magnolias (*Magnolia tripetala* and *Magnolia macrophylla*), with three-foot-long leaves and spring flowers
- Catalpa (*Catalpa bignonioides*), which has rounded leaves eight inches long and showy clusters of white flowers
- Empress tree (*Paulownia tomentosa*), which is not reliably hardy but so far has survived three winters at the zoo. Although this tree may die back to the ground during a harsh winter, it can resprout and grow 20 feet in one year. It has huge heart-shaped leaves twice the size of a catalpa
- Italian arum (*Arum italicum*), an unusual perennial with long arrowhead-shaped leaves that are evergreen in winter but die down in summer

- Plume poppy (*Macleaya cordata*), a fast-spreading perennial that can reach eight feet high, and bearing lush plumed flowers and eight-inch-long, lobed leaves that are furry white beneath
- Giant reed (*Arundodonax*), an ornamental grass that can tower up to 18 feet high and fill out into massive clumps

The landscaping surrounding the paddocks for the African plains animals looks very much like African savanna, right out of a Tarzan movie. All around the animals of China exhibit, next to the gorillas, you'll see plants from northern Asia that give you a better idea of where these animals originated.

If animals are grazing on the landscaping, Krock must be sure the plants are not toxic to any primates or ungulates. You will see that the tree canopies end just inches away from the big male giraffe's outstretched neck. But baby cheetahs are harder to keep away from the plants. "Baby cheetahs, who have a lot of extra energy, will pick a different clump of ornamental grass every day and chew it down to the ground. Fortunately, the grasses do resprout," Krock says.

In the bird house, a number of exhibits include plants in the bird enclosures. "Birds chew on the leaves and fly onto the branches, so they can be hard on plants. But they also take care of the small pest problems by eating white fly, aphids, scale, and spider mites. We never have to spray," Krock said.

(See also: Cleveland Zoological Society entry in General Horticultural Organizations, chapter 4.)

Cleveland Metroparks Zoo RainForest

(3900 Brookside Park Dr., Cleveland, 44109; 661-6500; admission fee; tickets available at the gate or from Ticketmaster, 241-5555)

This exhibit is the Metropark's jewel—for plants as well as animals. It re-creates the ever-diminishing rain forest areas of the world where a wealth of plant and animal species are threatened with extinction. The RainForest exhibit also represents horticultural pioneering at its best. It contains 10,000 live plants of 360 different varieties, including common and rare tropicals, orchids, bromeliads (a group of plants that grow on trees for support), cocoa trees, and vanilla vines.

"There is no other exhibit like this large-scale combination of live plants and animals within a 15-state area," Krock said. "The RainForest is a unique experience the public has never had a chance to see before. We are using high-tech graphics, Walt Disney effects, and fiber optics so lightning will flash and rain will fall beside the walks. In most areas, light levels will be fairly high so the plants should grow for five to six years before we have to replace them or they get too tall for the 35-foot roof. We use biological controls for pest problems, like beneficial insects [that prey upon or parasitize plant pests] and spot-spraying with nontoxic Bt [a bacterial disease of caterpillars], light horticultural oil [a nontoxic petroleum oil that coats and kills pests], or Safer's insecticidal soap [nontoxic soap made of fatty acids that kill soft-bodied insects]. (For more information on natural pest control, see Rodale's *Chemical-Free Yard and Garden*, 1991, Rodale Press, Emmaus, PA.)

You can also identify the plants; the exhibit resembles an overgrown ruin area throughout which a researcher went tagging plants with their common and botanical names. Volunteers can explain about rain forest plants of particular economic importance, such as fruits, woods, and fibers.

The plants are a combination of ornamental tropicals (such as black olive and fig trees used commonly for interior plantscaping) and unique flowering specimens (such as orchids that are rotated in and out of the exhibit as they come in and out of bloom). In the southeast corner, where butterflies emerge from their cocoons, you'll find nectar-producing plants such as passion vine and Egyptian star, which require extra light from overhead lamps. The floor plants grow in a peat-based growers' mix, not true soil, and those growing on the wall are rooted in carpet fiber and fed nutrients through a computerized watering and fertilizer system. It's an amazing assortment of plants and techniques brought together in an extraordinary exhibit.

Chagrin Valley Herb Society Garden
(Geauga County Public Library, Bainbridge Branch, 17222 Snyder Rd., Chagrin Falls, 44023; 543-5611)

Just outside the Geauga County Public library entrance you will find a small herb garden that is charming. Take a few minutes to look closely. This garden, designed by Karen Colini and planted and maintained by the Chagrin Valley Herb Society, consists of eight beds raised with timbers. It is the first phase of what is hoped will be a larger garden project.

The garden beds employ geometric patterns, a traditional way to design herb gardens. One bed is planted to resemble a wagon wheel, with spokes dividing the area into four quadrants devoted to different kinds of herbs and flowers. Another bed is filled with mints; free-ranging silver variegated pineapple mint—which spreads with abandon—fills the entire bed except in strategic locations where green-leafed mints remain in clumps.

The garden abounds with unusual herbs, including Florence fennel, chamomile, horehound, and angelica, and also fragrant plants such as scented geraniums. Especially attractive is the silver and blue bed, which combines plants with silver foliage—such as 'Silver Mound' artemisia, silver santolina, silver lamb's-ears, and dusty-miller—with blue-flowered plants, such as blue ageratum, salvia, and comfrey.

"The idea for the herb garden actually came first, and then

the Chagrin Valley Herb Society formed to create and work in it," said Kathy Catani, garden founder. "We now have about forty active members participating. One of the members is a librarian who knew nothing about gardening but seemed to be the one we always conferred with about the garden. Now she goes out and pulls weeds at lunch and has put in a couple of herb gardens at her own home. After a while, we made her an honorary member."

(See also: Plant Societies, chapter 4.)

Cleveland Museum of Art, Fine Arts Garden and Interior
(11150 East Blvd., University Circle, Cleveland, 44106; 421-7340; free admittance)

You find traces of gardens where you least expect to see them. Such is the case with the Cleveland Museum of Art. The Art Museum is located at one end of the Fine Arts Garden, a strolling area designed in the early 1900s by the landscape architecture firm of S. Olmsted Brothers of Brookline, Massachusetts. Garden areas circle a lagoon and include intriguing European-style pleached sycamore trees, which are pruned to have a flat-topped, interwoven, ceiling-like look. The general layout and the pleached trees remain from Olmsted's original garden and create an elegant setting for the museum building. Most of the garden has been cleared to make it a safer place to stroll—90 percent of the original shrubs have been taken out, and the remaining trees have had their lower branches removed so they do not create hiding places. Still, the Fine Arts Garden remains an oasis of greenery in the middle of the city.

Near the garden and elsewhere around the museum are about a dozen American elms, the few survivors of an attack of Dutch elm disease several decades ago. Also, there are interesting collections of cherry and crab apple trees, some quite rare, but it's difficult to tell one from another because they aren't labeled. Regardless, May and June are wonderful times to visit, as the bulbs and flowering trees produce an abundance of flowers.

Inside the museum, you'll find many flowers and conservatory plants that complement the season and the art displays. One week a month in the north lobby, you'll find a large flower arrangement crafted by volunteers from the Women's Council of the Cleveland Museum of Art. Elsewhere, plants are used to help guard the artwork.

"Plants keep the public back away from the exhibits. They hide the mechanics of the displays and guide the public through the right corridors," said Leon Santamary, former museum horticulturist. "Sometimes plants become part of the show. I tried to match the spirit of each show with the appropriate plant—like papyrus for the Egyptian exhibit, exotic cacti for the Picasso exhibit, bamboos and palms for Japanese exhibits."

Another special feature you will see from time to time are lavish pots of flowering orchids—*Cymbidium* orchids from November to February, and smaller botanical species in the summer. "We're unique from other art museums because we have our own greenhouse and can maintain a large collection of orchids—all of which have been donated to us by people in the area," Santamary said. The horticultural staff rejuvenates the plant collection by taking cuttings when the older plants begin to take a beating. They use cold frames for forcing bulbs into bloom.

In the heart of the museum, a garden court stretches up 25 feet high and provides a home for large tropical palms, fig trees, and rubber trees—huge old specimens that have seen decades come and go inside the museum.

Cleveland Museum of Natural History

(Wade Oval, Cleveland, 44106; 231-4600; admission fee; garden tours available with advance reservation)

As at the zoo, the link here between animals and plants is a natural. At the Museum of Natural History, native plants are cultivated in open courtyards within the museum. One garden is in a woodland; the other is open and in sun. Both include plants from different habitats (environments of different types of soil, watering, or light in which certain plants usually live).

Jim Bissell, curator of botany, said, "We created these gardens for minimal maintenance and now find that a lot of people come to see them because they are gardens that you can leave pretty much alone. It's funny how well accepted that idea is today. When we started these gardens 20 years ago, people used to complain because they thought we had run out of money and hadn't finished."

The first garden you'll see upon entering the main lobby is the Thelma and Kent Smith Environmental Courtyard, which is a riot of color in late summer as the prairie species take over. If you look closely at plant labels, you will find unusual native species from the northern hardwood forest, such as yellow birch (*Betula lutea*) and mountain maple (*Acer spicatum*). You'll also find more common plants that you may have heard about but never knew what they looked like, including elderberry (a fruit), goldenseal (a medicinal plant), and horsetail (*Equisetum hyemale*), the pioneer source of scouring brushes. Some of the species here are interesting simply to watch grow and develop.

"We found a neat phenomenon in the prairie area where big bluestem and Indian grass grows. Grasses are supposed to be wind pollinated but we saw that when the flowers are covered with dew before the sun hits them in the morning, the bees will pollinate them like crazy. They carry away pollen by the bucketload," Bissell said.

The second garden, located off the dinosaur gallery, is the Perkins Wildlife Memorial and Woods Garden. Most of the plants are clustered within a circular path that leads past animal cages. Because the area is shaded, its main display comes in spring. One section exhibits bog plants such as the very early blooming, heat-generating skunk cabbage and golden-flowered marsh marigold. Another is devoted to mixed mesophytic forest, with sugar maple, beech, oak, black cherry, witch hazel, sassafras, and tulip trees, and spring-blooming trilliums, Virginia bluebells, liverworts, and violets. A third section is devoted to such plants as Kentucky coffee tree, Chinquapin oak, bladdernut, trilliums, wild hyacinth, and trout lily.

Eastman Reading Garden

(Cleveland Public Library, 325 Superior Ave., Cleveland, 44114; 623-2800 [Because of library construction, the garden will be closed from October 1993 until sometime in 1995])

A couple blocks east of Public Square (which in itself is worth a wander through to see the informally pruned taxus hedges, fountain, and flowering trees) is a garden in which you can truly relax. It's the Eastman Reading Garden, part of the main branch of the Cleveland Public Library. Because it is enclosed in an encircling wall of greenery with tall buildings looming on either side, the garden feels especially peaceful and secluded given its proximity to bustling traffic.

The garden was established in 1937, converted from an unkempt city park to a place for outdoor reading. It was stocked with racks of books and magazines during library hours. The open-air access to the library collection didn't last long, though, because there was no way to control traffic flow through the area. In 1959, civic leaders took the garden in another direction by landscaping it with flowering trees and ivy, adding ornamental gates, a sundial, and wall fountain. The garden was renovated again in 1982 and decked out in new paving, raised beds for sweet-gum shade trees, a new fountain, and crab apples 'Dorothea' and 'Redbud'. The gates are still in place and are open from 9 a.m. to 5 p.m. from spring through fall.

Falconskeape Gardens
(7359 Branch Rd., Medina, 44256; 723-4966; admission fee)

The gardens at Falconskeape are lovely in spring when the huge collection of over six hundred varieties of lilacs and eighty varieties of crab apples are in bloom. These plants were developed through hybridizing by the late Father John Fiala, a lilac collector and author of *Lilacs: The Genus Syringa* (1988, Timber Press, Portland, OR).

"The Gardens began," Fiala explained, "way back when I was a child and used to help an elderly aunt, who, because of her illness, had me come to help in her large garden. She knew all the plants by their Latin names, had magnificent borders of delphiniums, roses, annuals that rivaled those seen in seed catalogs! . . . When I was twelve, I wrote to Arie den-Boer, then the famous horticulturist who was transforming the Des Moines, Iowa, Waterworks Grounds into an arboretum of all the then-available flowering crab apples. As a country lad, I knew very little about flowering crab apples. He wrote to me, sent scionwood for grafting and I was off on a lifetime adventure with Flowering Crabs. . . . Lilacs stole my heart away before I was twenty-one. I read all about them, obtained the best of grandmother's bushes, planted my own lilac walk and began hybridizing the best of the newest."

In other parts of the garden, you can see tree peonies,

daylilies, herbs, and roses, as well as Falcon Lake, which provides a picturesque view of water, fields, and woods nearby. (See also: Specialty Growers, chapter 3; Friends of Falconskeape Gardens entry in General Horticultural Organizations, chapter 4.)

The Garden Center of Greater Cleveland

(11030 East Blvd., University Circle, Cleveland, 44106; 721-1600; self-guided tour brochures available; free admittance; garden always open)

The Garden Center is a display garden designed on a smaller scale, making it easy to walk through and enjoy or to take new ideas home from. It is also frequently the site of wedding parties lined up waiting for their turn to take wedding photos, artists capturing scenes with paint or photographs, and occasional Garden Center parties that spill out onto the grounds.

You can learn about good gardening practices from the example the grounds set. Note how the formal clipped hedges are narrower at the top so that no part of the plant is shaded. Look closely at the perennial gardens where green L-shaped English link-stakes hold up floppy plants. "You can hook any number of these stakes together and loop them around a plant, preferably before, but even after, the stem flops," horticulturist Robin Siktberg said.

Check out how mulch is layered around trees that are growing in the lawn. "We put bark mulch around the trees to keep down mower damage and give the tree roots a small space where they are not competing with grass," Siktberg said. "But we only put mulch on two inches deep and don't touch the trunk."

You also will see many excellent plants that are not used enough in our area. Some are labeled, but label-snatching seems to be a popular sport in that neighborhood and labels frequently disappear. A few plants that grow on these grounds may not be hardy enough to survive long if you plant them further from the lake.

For more information on the gardens, ask at the front desk for self-guiding tour brochures. For the history of The Garden Center, see their book, *Fifty Years of Growing and Serving: 1930 to 1980.*

(See also: Adult Education, Children's Gardening Programs, Horticultural Therapy, Garden Libraries, and Special Events, chapter 2; Specialty Growers, chapter 3; General Horticultural Organizations, chapter 4.)

Following are some of the specific garden areas within The Garden Center grounds:

Western Reserve Herb Society Garden

This large herb garden, one of the finest in the country, was designed by landscape architect Elsetta Barnes in 1964. It includes a Tudor knot garden (a formal garden with clipped herbs that form intricate, interwoven geometric patterns), as well as culinary, medicinal, dye, fragrance, trial, and historic rose sections. Between brick walkways, the herb beds interweave flowers, foliage, and specimen plants to create a tapestry of colors and textures.

"It seemed reasonable for the garden to cover the interests of our members, which, on inquiry, I discovered were all aspects of herb gardening. I could not picture one large garden including such a mixture of plantings, and thus evolved the functional groupings," Barnes said.

What you won't know, unless you visit the garden on Tuesday or Thursday mornings when Herb Society volunteers are working there, is the amount of labor and love that goes into keeping everything just-so in this garden. Before the garden was developed, there were doubts about whether a volunteer organization could finance and maintain a garden of this scale. Now, after nearly thirty years, the industrious Herb Society has it heavily endowed, mostly from the proceeds of annual autumn herb fairs. How the Herb Society and their garden have risen from modest beginnings to national acclaim is documented in *A History of the Western Reserve Unit of the Herb Society of America: 1942–1992*, written by Elizabeth Scher and Jenifer Richter and published by the Western Reserve Herb Society for the Unit's fiftieth anniversary.

(See also: Plant Societies, chapter 4.)

Mary Ann Sears Swetland Rose Garden

This garden replicates a formal Roman rose garden enclosed in a clipped evergreen border. A series of angular rose beds, each devoted to a different color of rose, surround an octagonal marble fountain. The garden seems simple and serene; this is by careful design. It replaced an older, unmaintained rose garden that was full of brambles and weeds—no one wanted that to happen again.

Evans Reading Garden

The Evans Reading Garden serves as an extension of the large Garden Center library. It invites visitors to stop with a book under a lengthy vine-covered pergola/summerhouse or on benches situated in shady nooks. It is also a place to find unusual plants such as Alleghany pachysandra, Himalayan sarcococca, and Russian arborvitae, some of which were collected on the worldwide travels of the garden's sponsor, Betty Evans.

Japanese Garden

This garden, a naturalistic miniature mountainscape, is downhill from the Reading Garden. Walk through a wrought-iron gate along a stone path to a wisteria-draped trellis, a tea garden, and a dry waterfall torrent created of rocks and clipped shrubbery. Covering the slopes and surrounding the tea garden are Oriental plants such as dwarf Mugo pine, Japanese holly and maple, and evergreen azalea. This garden was designed by David Slawson, former Clevelander and author of *Secret Teachings in the Art of Japanese Gardens* (1987, Kodansha International, Tokyo).

Wildflower Garden

To the west of the Japanese Garden is the most recent addition to these grounds. For many years before it was actually developed into a garden, the late John Milchalko, former commissioner of shade trees for the city of Cleveland, dumped tons of leaves there, making the soil rich and fertile. Milchalko helped spearhead volunteer efforts to relocate wildflowers that were on construction sites to the safety of the ravine. The Garden Center continued where the volunteer efforts left off when the city leased them the property in 1987.

Over the past ten years, the ravine has been converted from a brush-covered no man's land into a woodland glade woven with paths, seats, and flowers. Native wildflowers such as wild columbine, trillium, and Solomon's-seal, and wildflower-like species from other countries, such as Siberian bugloss, Bethlehem sage, and Lenten rose spread in abundance up and down the ravine slopes. For more details on this garden, you can purchase a trail guide at The Garden Center.

The Interior

If you tire of being outdoors, view the grounds from the glass-walled Garden Center building, which houses Garden

Center activities, the extensive library, and occasional educational or art displays. The building also holds garden shows, including the Christmas and spring shows.

Gardenview Horticultural Park

(16711 Pearl Rd., Rte. 42, Strongsville, 44136; 238-6653; non-members can visit on Saturdays and Sundays; admission fee charged for nonmembers)

Gardenview Horticultural Park, a surprising, tranquil garden hidden in a commercial area of Strongsville, contains expansive English cottage gardens and traditional perennial borders unlike any other garden in this area. The six acres of artistic gardens, through which you can wander on winding paths, back up to ten additional acres devoted to an arboretum of crab apples and spring bulbs.

The garden has been the lifelong creation of Henry Ross, who has bartered and traded for an astonishing number of rare plants and has single-handedly developed and maintained the garden. Ross has a special touch with plants; his gardens combine some of the area's most creative annual displays. Especially impressive past combinations have included:

• Large white flowering tobacco plants with modern compact white flowering cultivars at their feet
• Tropical five-foot-tall cannas with golden variegated leaves, orange flowers, and red buds with burgandy-leaf coleus, red-plumed cockscomb, and purple-stemmed ornamental kale
• Ruby-stemmed Swiss chard with pink double-flowered impatiens

Some areas of this park have a calculated impromptu look. In one undeveloped meadow off the main path, wonderful leafless flower stalks of light orchid lycoris (*Lycoris squa-*

migera) flowers bloom beautifully without any obvious sign of human intervention. They stand out—a bold color amid autumn grasses.

In the midst of these colorful displays you will find rare plants that nurseries across the United States have come to covet. Look for hybrid Lenten roses and hostas, variegated comfrey and variegated Siberian bugloss (*Brunnera macrophylla*), as well as simply unusual plants such as deciduous ginger, bear's-breeches, and Italian arum.

Of the garden, Ross writes, "Gardenview was designed as, and is, not only a magnificent example of glorious 'real gardens'; but an inspiration to those visiting it. Containing primarily very rare, uncommon and unusual plants, it is made up of about thirty individual gardens, . . . all informal and casual, fitting together into one picture, like pieces of a puzzle. Its purpose is not only to provide pleasure to those viewing it, but to inspire them to 'go home and do likewise'. It provides not only numerous examples of planting combinations; but layout ideas as well. It is a 'real gardeners' garden and not an extravaganza for the general non-gardening public. It is also intended to make people realize that ornamental 'real' gardening is a pleasure and a joy and to inspire people to create and enjoy 'real gardens' and to abandon the idea of wanting—and settling for—a low-maintenance landscaped area made up of green lumps which require little or preferably NO care; because they have been brainwashed into believing that real gardening is unpleasant work and should be avoided."

In his philosophy and in his life's work, Ross displays a European perspective that proves enlightening as you peruse the grounds of Gardenview.

(See also: General Horticultural Organizations, chapter 4.)

Garfield Park Nature Center, Metroparks

(Garfield Park Reservation, 11350 Broadway Ave., Garfield Hts., 44125; 341-3152)

This Reservation has one of the largest cultivated gardens in the Metropark system. The spring wildflower garden is a must-see, but you also can walk down a garden path clothed on either side in hummingbird and butterfly flowers. The creatures fly back and forth across the walk as they feed. In addition, there is an herb garden, a composting display, and a rock garden (which is in the peak of bloom in July).

Because this collection of gardens is so large, the nature center is always looking for volunteers to help maintain them. Call 341-3152 for more information.

Goldsmith Garden at Hale Farm

(2626 Oak Hill Rd., Bath, 44210; 575-9137; open Wednesday to Sunday, May to October and during December; admission fee)

The Goldsmith Garden at the Western Reserve Historical Society's Hale Farm and Village can take you back to the pioneer era when people were much more reliant on their gardens than today. Pioneer gardens provided fruit, vegetables, flowers, medicine, cloth dyes, and fragrances, all of which you will see in sections of this elaborate garden. To supplement garden varieties, a field behind is devoted to an apple orchard and to large field crops, including potatoes, squash, and corn.

Western Reserve Historical Society volunteer Kathleen Van Devere designed the Goldsmith Garden using an 1830s garden plan and pre-1850s diaries, journals, and manuscripts. As was typical in that era, she enclosed the garden with a tall stockade fence in the back and picket fence in the front, both essential for keeping out marauding animals. Like the Cahoon Memorial Rose Garden, the Goldsmith Garden has a round central focal point, which may have been a sundial or water garden on the original 1830s plan. Unlike the rose garden, however, the beds here are four feet wide, rectangular, and raised—a layout popular among modern intensive gardeners because its center can be reached from either side without stepping into the bed and compressing the soil. According to Van Devere's research, early garden designers also were concerned with other issues we ponder today, such as providing for a succession of bloom (a sequence of flowers to bloom through the summer), easy-to-grow flowers (quite similar to our low-maintenance emphasis), and flowers that bloom for a longer period of time.

Van Devere said that people "tend to be pleasantly surprised because the garden is so sophisticated for a village of this size. But that's the way higher-income families of that time gardened. If you want to see how families in the lower economic scale gardened, look at the herbs growing by the Saltbox. They are rows of things put in the ground."

Cheryl Kukwa, the grounds and gardens specialist at Hale Farm, has been surprised by the numbers of plants available to early gardeners. Historical society literature lists 41 cultivars of apple trees available. Among the vegetables and herbs early pioneers in this area grew were sweet potatoes, cucumbers, turnips, peas, caraway seeds, cabbage, lettuce, beans (five kinds, including tropical castor oil, which is not a true bean at all), asparagus, rhubarb, artichoke, gourds, turnips (or large radishes), four kinds of squash, three kinds of corn (including black, popcorn, and broomcorn, which was used to make fibrous brooms), six kinds of potatoes, rutabaga, onion, pepper, tomato, peppergrass, broccoli, carrots, cauliflower, beets, purple eggplant, parsley, sage, savory, sweet marjoram, and hops.

Among flowers, diversity is again amazing. Early settlers had 60 kinds of verbena, chrysanthemums, spiderwort (*Tra-*

descantia), peonies, dahlias, irises, carnations, pinks, sunflowers, an assortment of bulbs, and azaleas. Determining the exact species or cultivars grown a century ago, though, is a difficult proposition.

"Every year I get two or three calls from people who want to know how historically accurate the garden is," said Van Devere. "I can only answer that we tried to validate the kinds of plants used, and how they were used, but did not confirm the plant species. As we learn more about what was available at that time and find modern-day sources, we hope that we can upgrade species and cultivars within the present planting plan. But some of the early species and varieties of plants are lost forever, which is a real shame."

For more information on the Hale Farm, look for *The Jonathan Hale Farm: A Chronicle of the Cuyahoga Valley* (by John J. Horton, Publication 116 of the Western Reserve Historical Society). For more information on historic cultivars, contact the Seed Saver's Exchange, a nonprofit organization devoted to trading and preserving old-fashioned plants, at Rural Route 3, Box 239, Decorah, IA 52101.

Haymaker Parkway
(Rte. 59 from Longmere St. to Willow St. in Kent; organized by the Kent Environmental Council; pick up brochures at Kent City Hall or Chamber of Commerce)

The State Route 59 Bypass in Kent, a one-mile stretch called Haymaker Parkway, has become home for a network of gardens—mixed beds of perennials, ground covers, and shrubs with hundreds of shade and evergreen trees. The result of grassroots networking, it's worth a visit when you are in the neighborhood. The plantings—the first of which were developed in 1985—have been financed by the fund-raising efforts of the Kent Environmental Council. There are already eight large perennial beds and gardens surrounding the city hall, and more gardens on the way.

One of the most unusual planting areas, designed by Dr. Joan Sturtevant, co-owner of Gateway Gardens, is the side hill of city hall. It includes over three thousand bulbs and seven kinds of ornamental grasses. There also are drifts of popular perennials such as Salvia 'East Friesland', lobelia, pinks (*Dianthus* species), bergenia, and lilyturf (*Liriope* species) interplanted with twelve cultivars of heather and five kinds of junipers. Near the front walk to city hall are over eighty old-fashioned roses, a thousand bulbs, and more mixed plantings of perennials, trees, and shrubs.

Among the woody plants, look for more unusual specimens such as the smoke tree, Japanese pagoda tree (*Sophora japonica*), purple and tricolor beech, tree lilacs, sapphire berry (*Symplocos paniculata*), fragrant epaulette tree (*Pterostyrax hispidus*), and false spirea (*Sorbaria sorbifolia*).

Hiram Community Gardens: Hurd Memorial Garden
(corner of Hayden and Bancroft streets in Hiram; garden tours available by advance reservation with Jamie Barrow, P.O. Box 402, Hiram, 44234)

One of the best public gardens in this area is not large, but every inch of it is beautifully used. The Hurd Memorial Garden on the campus of Hiram College is a Victorian garden— a Perennial Plant Association Honor Award winner—that was designed by Valerie Strong.

"The garden was created because the old Hurd house had been torn down against the wishes of the community. To placate them, Jamie Barrow [a local garden enthusiast] who had organized the installation and maintenance of other Hiram gardens, decided to turn the property into a garden. It was dedicated to the Hurd family, two generations of doctors who were in Hiram from the late 1800s to about 1960. Now that the garden is maturing, it has made up for a whole lot of bad feelings. Hiram has a lot of gardens, but most are contemplative rather than display," Strong said.

As was common in Victorian times, Strong divided the long, narrow corner lot that the garden occupies into three gardens: a medicinal garden on the north end, a yellow garden in the center, and a wilderness garden to the south. You can enter through a vine-covered arbor and walk looping trails that open up to exciting new views around each turn. There are Victorian plants such as bayberry, spirea, lilacs, catmint, phlox, sunflower, purple loosestrife, ornamental grasses, and cleome; some of the best of popular new cultivars of older plants such as coneflower 'Goldsturm', threadleaf coreopsis 'Moonbeam', and sedum 'Autumn Joy'; and some unique specimens such as a cut-leaf sumac and weeping mulberry (also popular in Victorian times). Secluded benches scattered throughout invite you to rest. Strong tends to group each type of perennial plant and many of the shrubs in masses so that they make a big impact. The garden is well groomed and full of color throughout the seasons, even in winter, when the ornamental grasses stand golden against the snow.

In the medicinal garden, beds swirl around a Victorian urn; a crescent of foundation stones saved from an early Hiram building and old Victorian lampposts extend along the walk. "The garden is arranged so it is closed off by shrubbery from the street, which makes it seem private even though it's public. It is surrounded by a fence that is a replica of the perching fence that enclosed the original campus. Couples used to sit there on the top board—a modern-day drive-in," said Strong.

If you join up with a garden tour, you can also see eight other, smaller, gardens around Hiram: Copper Beech, Bonney Castle, Pendleton, Century House, Missionary Garden,

Mahan House, Piney Woods, and Horticulture Garden.
(See also: General Horticultural Organizations, chapter 4.)

The Holden Arboretum
(9500 Sperry Rd., Kirtland, 44060; 946-4400; admission fee for non-members; closed Mondays)

The Holden Arboretum's 3,100 acres of land make it one of the largest arboreta in the country and a great asset for our community. You can get a feel for the expanse of all this land by driving to the arboretum on the newly rerouted Sperry Road, a replacement for the old pothole-ridden gravel road. The new road winds through rolling landscape that the old road kept hidden.

"We had always been so close to the old road that we never considered that we could back off from it until we had a master plan designed by a Pittsburgh landscape architect. He said we had to get rid of that straight line, and picked a new route that gives a wonderful view of the landscape through the east branch of the Chagrin Valley to the top of Little Mountain. It really shows the vastness of the area," said Holden Arboretum director Eliot Paine.

(See also: Adult Education, Children's Gardening Programs, Horticultural Therapy, Garden Libraries, and Special Events, chapter 2; Specialty Growers, chapter 3; General Horticultural Organizations, chapter 4.)

If you focus your sightseeing, you can see the garden areas of the Arboretum in a single visit. Look for the following:

Myrtle S. Holden Wildflower Garden
This five-acre garden of Ohio plants starts beneath a high canopy of sugar maples and stretches out of the woods into rockery, prairie, fen, and bog plantings. The collection

includes over five hundred species, most of which the Arboretum staff have propagated in Holden's greenhouses.

The plants, which grow in natural groupings along winding trails, pack the woodland with color from April to May. The prairie takes over in summer. The bog garden is especially interesting because the plants, including pitcher plants that catch and consume insects, grow on top of acidic water covered with a layer of sphagnum moss. A fen is a similar boggy area, but with alkaline water and a different set of plants. The rockery area contains species that grow naturally in dunes, sand, or rock areas—including endangered plants like the Lakeside daisy, one of the rarest plants in Ohio. The plants are labeled with different colored tags according to how rare they are.

"The whole thrust of this garden is to model habitat communities—to duplicate soil, moisture, and light conditions— in which these plants naturally grow. We don't expect to save endangered species by planting them in our garden, but we teach people about them and learn the basics of their biology that land managers may some day need. We also send the seeds and spores to the Federal Seed Repository, where they are maintained and preserved for the future," Brian Parsons, garden curator, said.

Display Garden Landscape Collection

This area just south of the visitor's center is more of a working and idea area than a beautiful garden, but in it you will see some of the better landscape plants for our region. "We do have collections of single items like viburnums, lilacs, and a new daylily area, but we also are trying to show how different plants will grow together and how to combine various textures and colors," said Jim Mack, superintendent of grounds. For example, one grouping uses a paperbark maple with a backdrop of lilacs to show how well the peeling cinnamon-colored bark shows up against a curtain of green.

Rhododendron Garden

This three-acre collection of rhododendrons, artfully arranged beneath ancient trees, including a 350-year old white oak and a red oak 100 years its junior, is well worth hiking to in late May and early June. Some of the rhododendrons are over fifty years old; others are new hybrids developed by local breeders, including Peter Girard, Dr. David Leach, the late Anthony Shammarello, and the late Paul Bosley. This garden also features famous earlier types, such as Dexter rhododendrons (Massachusetts, 1920s), Ghent Hybrid azaleas (Belgium, early 1800s), and Knap Hill azaleas (England, 1870s). These rhododendrons and azaleas flower prolifically amid related companions of heather, heath, mountain laurel, mountain andromeda, blueberries, and leucothoe.

Lantern Court

(9203 Kirtland-Chardon Rd., Kirtland, 44060; gardens open Wednesdays; tours on some Sundays; pay admission at the main Holden Arboretum building; house can be reserved for meetings by nonprofit organizations)

This lovely 25-acre garden, on the former estate of Warren and Maud Corning, was built in the early 1930s. The gardens were originally designed by local landscape architect Donald Gray, but have been expanded and refined over the years. Mr. Corning was an avid plant collector and some of his original plantings remain, including daffodils, tree peonies, primroses, pines, hemlocks, oaks, and a weeping willow. Tom Yates, the garden superintendent for the last twenty years, has done his share of seeking out new cultivars and unusual plants for the gardens, adding to the start Corning made.

As you enter the grounds, which are around the corner from the Arboretum entrance, you will see the Corning formal garden. Its terraced rose beds and geometrical cutting gardens stretch between a hemlock hedge, clipped yews, and a long English-style perennial border. The small details, such as tiny blue lobelia plants flowering between the steps that link rose and cutting gardens, are charming.

Along the drive and across the front of the property, flowing island beds of spring flowering bulbs, perennials, and flowering shrubs are molded to the contour of the slope. The woods creep along the drive on the front (west) side of the house close to a small arcade-like orangery (an early greenhouse used to grow citrus trees). Nearby, a shallow boggy ravine is filled with plants that like wet feet. Look for rare species such as pitcher plants, Western skunk cabbage, and exotic primroses. Beside the ravine runs a shaded primrose walk and rock garden with dwarf conifers, heather, and small alpine plants.

Switch gears by taking a path through informal gardens. It lies east of the house and will lead you through a wildflower- and hosta-planted woodland behind the house to a fern garden and steep hemlock-clothed ravine with a dramatic waterfall.

Lake County Farmpark

(8800 Chardon Rd., Kirtland, 44094; 800-366-FARM; admission fee)

Lake County Farmpark combines an emphasis on animals with the accompanying agricultural practices (haymaking, grain harvesting, threshing), gardens of old-fashioned vegetables (dragon tongue beans, broomcorn, grain amaranth, and coriander), and fruit orchards and berry fields.

"We have blueberries, strawberries, grapes, and raspberries

that you can eat by invitation during regular tours. We also let schoolchildren sample the honey straight from the honeycomb in our apiary. We pass the honey around and, when everyone has their mouth full, I ask them if they know how honey is made. A lot of full-mouthed kids are shocked to learn bees take in the nectar, and then regurgitate it to make honey," says Tim Malinich, horticulture specialist.

In 1992, Lake County Farmpark added a new horticultural center in their Planter's Overlook area. Eventually it will be filled with hands-on projects such as seed sowing and transplanting for pre-organized groups, a hydroponics (growing plants in water instead of soil) display, and an exhibit explaining how plants grow and develop.

(See also: Adult Education, chapter 2.)

Lake Erie Nature and Science Center
(28728 Wolf Rd., Bay Village, 44140; 871-2900)

This privately operated nature center, located in the Metropark's Huntington Reservation, has a small nature garden developed by its women's board. You can stroll through the garden to see native wildflowers and non-natives (all labeled) that can attract wildlife to home landscapes. "One of our big drawing cards is that families with young children can come here and see the whole facility in an hour, and then go do whatever they have to do that particular day," said Larry Richardson, director.

The Nature and Science Center also offers wildflower walks in the surrounding 108-acre park, tree-identification programs, and other plant-oriented field studies or classes. They have a spring plant sale called the Spring Thing, and offer annual and perennial plants and wildflowers, some of which are local.

Lake View Cemetery

(12316 Euclid Avenue, East Cleveland/Cleveland Heights, 44106;
421-2665; self-guided tour available at office)

This cemetery, full of statues and monuments (including the burial place of President James Garfield), is also is a 285-acre arboretum. Originally developed in 1869 as a Victorian landscape park, its layout is true to those times: winding drives curve through a large park and over sloped ground that moves from the low-lying sandy areas toward the lake to the clay ridge in Cleveland Heights.

Like a museum, the grounds hold horticultural history and ancient trees—500 of which are labeled so you can appreciate them better. Because Lake View Cemetery was established during an era of extensive plant exploration in the Orient, it is a treasure-house of big Oriental species and other unusual woody plants, including:

• Rare Chinese species, such as paper bark maple (*Acer griseum*), Chinese toon (*Cedrela sinensis*), hupeh evodia (*Evodia hupehensis*), and Chinese maackia (*Maackia chinensis*)
• Tree giants like the 100-year-old Sargent's weeping hemlock (*Tsuga canadensis* 'Sargentii'), a Moses Cleaveland American beech, and tulip trees and white oaks
• Unusual trees, including a cut-leaf weeping sugar maple, double-flowered dogwood, and big-leaf magnolias
• Loads of beautiful flowering trees, such as redbud, buckeyes, crab apples and magnolias
• Over 100,000 bulbs on three-acre Daffodil Hill
(See also: Adult Education, chapter 2.)

Mary Elizabeth Garden, Lake County Nursery, Inc.

(5052 South Ridge Rd. [Rte. 84], Perry, 44081; 259-5571;
for more information contact Maria Pettorini)

The Mary Elizabeth Garden, named after the wife of Felix Zampini, the founder of Lake County Nursery, Inc., is a one-acre garden featuring over five hundred types of herbs and flowers grown by this wholesale nursery. Paths wind past thousands of spring bulbs, shade gardens of ferns and hostas, unusual conifers, perennial flowers, a waterfall and sunken garden, and many of the nursery's own cultivars.

(See also: Champion Garden Towne entry in Specialty Growers, chapter 3.)

Moldovan's Gardens

(Steve Moldovan, 38830 Detroit Rd., Avon, 44011; 934-4993;
open to the public during flowering season from May to August,
but the peak of daylily bloom is July 5th–15th)

Behind what appears to be an ordinary white house on the outskirts of Avon stretches a four-acre garden, a beautiful display area and breeding ground for hostas and daylilies developed by Steve Moldovan. Neat freeform garden beds sweep down the gentle incline of the long and relatively narrow yard. Here and there, masses of daylilies interweave with other perennials, including bellflowers, peonies, periwinkle, and pink-flowered lungwort, as well as annual flowers and dahlias.

The sunny beds are broken by specimen plants such as dwarf Japanese maple, roses, large oaks, magnolias, and small groves of maple trees. There are seats and sculpture interspersed throughout the main part of the garden, which stands out from the surrounding lawns and fields of corn and soybean. Also, an intriguing secret garden section lies just downhill from a reflecting pool and rock garden. Enter it through an opening in a wild bamboo thicket and find thousands of seedlings planted beyond.

Shady nooks provide the setting for Moldovan's hostas, a perennial grown primarily for its interesting leaves. Hostas also bloom, often in midsummer, sending up spikes of white or lavender flowers that can be fragrant. One hosta, called 'Corduroy', is especially eye-catching; its leaves are each over a foot long, making the plant more than four feet wide and high, and it holds up especially well into early September, when other hosta are fading.

You can see subtle signs that the area is a working garden. All the plants are labeled with aluminum tags and some of the seedpods are tagged as well.

(See also: Specialty Growers, chapter 3.)

Oberlin College Campus
(Oberlin, Lorain County; self-guided garden tour brochures available at the Oberlin College Inn, North Main St.; 775-1111)

A necklace of perennial gardens and mixed beds of woody plants stretches across the Oberlin College campus. It's an excellent display to check out in midsummer when the campus is quiet, according to William Salo, manager of grounds.

You can learn while you stroll if you buy a tour brochure, which tells the history of the college campus and points out examples of microclimates and hardiness variations. Because the campus was founded in 1833, it features wonderful big trees—some planted over 150 years ago. They're most notable in Tappan Square, the site of many early college buildings. A campus brochure notes, "Early settlers cut down the native trees, creating a field of stumps, and the area was for a time known as Stumpyville. Later the Square was enclosed by a hedgerow of Osage Orange, which remained until the 1880s." Since the original clearing of the Square, tree planting has become an annual event led, in early years, by ". . . students from the East, whose life had not been a constant warfare with trees."

The largest group of perennial gardens surrounds the Oberlin College Inn, where about a hundred different varieties of bulbs and flowers spread through eight gardens. Near the Allen Memorial Art Museum, you'll find a formal herb garden developed with a symmetrical display of evergreen herbs for winter color, and other herbs that shine in summer.

Oldest Stone House
(Lakewood Park, Bell and Lake avenues, Lakewood; 221-7343)

In the small enclosed area surrounding the Oldest Stone House, you can browse through an herb garden, the working and display site of the Oldest Stone House Herb Society. The L-shaped garden houses about fifty different kinds of herbs that the society harvests for their herbal projects. It ends in a rockport, where historical tombstones are interplanted with traditional herbs that represented loss or were used for embalming, such as santolina, lilies-of-the-valley, foxglove, southernwood, artemisia, and costmary.

"Overall, this garden is similar to the casual doorstep garden of an early dwelling in this area," said Sandy Koozer, curator of the Lakewood Historical Society.

(See also: Plant Societies, chapter 4.)

Rockefeller Park Greenhouse
(750 E. 88th St., Cleveland, 44108; 664-3103; free admittance; open daily; guided tours available with four-week advance reservation)

The Rockefeller Park Greenhouse, a working greenhouse for the city of Cleveland and, more recently, a public display garden, is attracting more visitors than ever before. It is a fun place to go, and it's free (though in some places not beautifully maintained because of city staff cuts). You can reach the greenhouse by driving north from Chester Avenue on Martin Luther King Jr. Drive through what remains (very little, unfortunately) of the Cultural Gardens.

At the greenhouse, four acres of outdoor gardens stretch north and south of the greenhouse range and parking lot. To the south, beyond a gazebo, are a mixture of different gardens (many donated by local organizations) that are collectively called the Peace Garden. There you can see interesting displays of globe artichokes, new annual cultivars, dahlias, and irises.

"Irises grow so much better here in the rich loose soil and more moderate climate. We're only about a quarter-mile from the lake," said iris breeder Tony Willott. "It's like a different world from where I live in Beachwood."

Four persimmon trees—two male, two female—bear a crop unusual in this area. "We had two trees that never fruited. Then two ladies from Seven Hills came in and said they had persimmon trees that flowered but never fruited. Since you need both male and female trees to have a crop, they donated their trees to us. Ever since then, we've had tons of fruit around the first fall frost," said Chris Jagelewski, horticulturist maintenance foreman.

To the north of the parking lot is a formal lawn area, the English Mall, that is backed by a wonderful rock-sculpted Japanese garden that you may have seen without knowing it— it is a frequent site of television interviews. Below the greenhouse is the Betty Ott Garden for the Blind, which contains plants that appeal to senses other than sight and offers a taped explanation of each area. It was renovated in 1992 by The Women's City Club.

Inside the greenhouse you'll find a world of tropical plants, orchids, cacti, fountains, and changing displays of lavishly massed flowers. The greenhouses are the remains of the old orchid growing range built by nineteenth-century philanthropist William J. Gordon. Around the turn of the century, John D. Rockefeller bought the property and added onto the greenhouse ranges. When Rockefeller quarreled with the city about unpaid taxes, he moved out of the area and left the greenhouse to the city. It became a working nursery, supplying other city parks with flowers and trees. In 1960 a tropical showroom and some of the outside gardens were added, and it began to attract visitors.

To keep up the present displays, Don Slogar, manager, encourages volunteer groups to help with planting or maintenance. Slogar has also helped start the Friends of the Cleveland Greenhouse, a nonprofit group that helps raise funds to support greenhouse activities (see General Horticultural Organizations, chapter 4).

"We can't justify the Greenhouse's existence by beauty alone. This has to be a people place, and it has become one. We have dozens of people here every day, from toddlers to seniors," said Slogar.

Rocky River Nature Center, Metroparks

(Rocky River Reservation, 24000 Valley Parkway, North Olmsted, 44070)

You will find three gardens here. One is devoted to flowers that attract butterflies and hummingbirds in summer. Another, the Ron Hauser Memorial Wildflower Garden, peaks in April and May but also contains a few summer-blooming native plants such as columbine, cardinal flower, blue lobelia, and closed gentian that stretch the blooming season. The third, a small herb garden, features plants that area settlers relied on for medicine, cooking, and hiding the odors of overly ripe meat and overly ripe people. Among the herbs you'll see here are sage, once used to help people digest greasy meats; chamomile, used then and now as a yellow dye, for tea, and as a hair rinse for blonds; and wormwood, strewn on dirt floors to repel fleas.

Sanctuary Marsh Nature Center, Metroparks
(North Chagrin Reservation, Buttermilk Falls Parkway, Mayfield Village, 44094; 473-3370)
There is an herb garden outside the nature center doorway and a spring wildflower garden nearby. A small garden of hummingbird flowers and bird-feeding shrubs stands outside the window where you can watch the animals at work during both summer and winter.

Sea World of Ohio
(1100 Sea World Dr., Aurora, 44202; 562-8101; admission fee)
You may think of Sea World as a special place to see whales, dolphins, and water shows, but there are lots of gardening ideas there, too, framing the animal life and other attractions.

"We landscape to entertain, to provide the feeling of fluid movement, since this is an aquatic park. We use pastel-tone flowers with white, which adds drama and is an underused color in most landscapes. Once you put in white, you find you can't do without it because it draws the eye and creates movement," said Deborah Davis, Sea World horticulturist.

The main display beds are filled with petunias, impatiens, begonias, and geraniums, all propagated in one of the Sea World greenhouses. A second greenhouse is devoted to raising exotic plants from seed. Some of these unusual plants crept into a recent Monster Marsh exhibit.

"When we were planning Monster Marsh, I went through every book I had and looked for flowers that looked prehistoric," Davis said. Some of the more spectacular plants she chose were tricolor amaranth, which looked like molten lava; perilla, a member of the mint family with purple and glistening leaves; and hops, which grew all over the place so it looked like a runaway monstery vine.

Other interesting gardens include Shark Encounter, with

sharp thorny plants and lots of rocks, and a total-access garden, which can be enjoyed by blind, wheelchair-bound, or other disabled people.

If you have any questions as you stroll the park (which is easy to enjoy even from a wheelchair), ask horticultural staff members—they wear the bright green shirts. You can also call Sea World directly or write.

(See also: Adult Education, chapter 2.)

Shaker Lakes Regional Nature Center
(2600 South Park Blvd., Shaker Heights, 44120; 321-5935)

When you drive into the parking lot of this nature center, you are greeted by a spectacular boardwalk that traverses a wetland area. Wander along this "All People's Trail" to see interesting marsh plants, blackbirds, water birds, muskrats, and other wildlife. Although less obvious, a wildflower garden is located to the east of the Nature Center building. This mature garden was started about twenty-five years ago by members of the Shaker Lakes Garden Club, who still maintain the area. "One of our biggest battles now is keeping out unwanted plants like periwinkle, pachysandra, and goutweed. We spend a lot of time pulling things out," said Linda Johnson, Nature Center volunteer and board member.

The Nature Center also offers environmental education classes for children and a spring plant sale.

(See also: Children's Gardening Programs, chapter 2; Specialty Growers, chapter 3.)

Silver Creek Farm
(7097 Allyn Rd., P.O. Box 254, Hiram, 44234; 562-4381; tours, group talks, and slide shows available)

Although this is not a show garden, you may enjoy seeing how an organic market garden operates. Silver Creek Farm, operated by Ted and Molly Bartlett, is certified organic by the Ohio Ecological Food and Farm Association, which means the produce is grown in a chemical-free environment and in a manner that safeguards the land. The Bartletts own 125 acres, much of which is woodlands held in a land trust. The fields are devoted to blueberries, squash, greens, peas, peppers, herbs, eggplant, beets, broccoli, garlic, and heirloom tomatoes.

You may have to walk past several fallow fields to reach the growing area. Although weeds can be seen between the raised, plastic-mulched beds, these are evidence that no herbicides touch the land. And the crops grow beautifully. The key, according to Molly Bartlett, is building the soil with livestock manure, creating a proper environment for beneficial bugs that eat other pests, and rotating crops so that different plant families follow in different spots, eliminating pest buildup.

"We use our own barnyard manure that has no livestock chemicals in it. It's very different from stable manures," said Bartlett. "Sometimes we grow companions together that benefit each other, like leeks with tomatoes. Earlier in spring we once had to dust the eggplants with diatomaceous earth (microscopical, prickly, sandlike particles harvested from marine algae), and that stopped most bugs; and we use Bt for cabbage loopers. I think if you could cover everything with Reemay (a brand of floating woven row covers) you could eliminate most problems, especially on young plants of cucumbers and watermelons."

The Bartletts encourage visitors to come for Farm Market, every Saturday, 10 a.m. to 4 p.m., from Mother's Day until New Year's Day. They kick off the spring season on Mother's Day by selling seedlings of heirloom tomatoes (herb seedlings and other speciality items are sold all summer long), offering sheep-shearing demonstrations, and harvesting exotic Oriental shiitake mushrooms, which they cultivate in their woods. They also have craft items—sheep skins, yarns, sweaters, maple syrup—and other gifts for sale all season long. You can also find their produce at the Food Co-op in University Circle, the Baricelli Inn, and at other restaurants and grocery stores selling organic produce.

(See also: Specialty Growers, chapter 3.)

Stan Hywet Hall

(714 N. Portage Path, Akron, 44303; 836-5533; admission fee; grounds tour available with advance reservation)

If you want to visit a garden that will impress and inspire, go to Stan Hywet Hall in Akron, the former estate of F. A. Seiberling, co-founder of Goodyear Tire and Rubber Company. The 70-acre landscape was developed beginning in 1911 by landscape architect Warren Manning, who helped design New York's Central Park. Although the gardens have changed over the years, the Stan Hywet Hall Board of Trustees is in the process of restoring the gardens to their original design.

The most recent renovation is the Walled English Garden, restored to its 1930 glory, an elaborate flowery design originally prepared by Ellen Shipman. Her garden included 1,500 flowers and bulbs flowering in white, pale yellow, pink, rose, blue, and lavender within a sunken brick-walled area.

Shipman was a genius at coordinating all these plants. The design is perfect. The rectangular garden includes a large reflecting pool and a statue with a fountain, both surrounded by walks and garden beds. In late summer, every bed blazes with tall airy asters and anemones, delphiniums, glads, phlox, and lower growing sedum and forget-me-not—all in full bloom without signs of late summer fatigue. This is possible, said garden volunteer Kathleen Van Devere, because plants are moved in and out of the garden following Shipman's plan. Signs of spring bloomers remain in the foliage of peonies, Siberian bugloss, and coralbells, which form strong edging lines that complement the brick walks and unify the garden.

It's easy to imagine the garden 70 years ago with women in swirling long dresses and gentlemen in suits tipping their hats during a garden party, or Gertrude Seiberling, wife of F.A. Seiberling and mother of six surviving children, taking a cup of tea out there in the peaceful surroundings. A poem by the lower entrance reads:

> A garden is a lovesome
> Thing God wot
> Rose Plot
> Fringed Pool
> Fern'd Grot
> The veriest school of peace and yet the
> fool contends that God is not God! In Gardens!
> When the eve is cool?
> Nay but I have a sign tis very sure God walks in mine.

A lot of labor is required to maintain this garden; part of the work is supplied by Akron Garden Club volunteers on Monday and Friday mornings.

The other gardens spread out from the grandiose Tudor Revival mansion built early in this century. As you enter through the main gate, you will see Manning's idea of a welcome: the great meadow lawn, which provides a foreground to distant views and a quiet informal space without the blaze of color and hard formal lines that make up a summer garden.

Manning sectioned the estate into individual areas. When you park, you will see the huge cutting gardens, now larger than Manning originally planned. They supply flowers for arrangements created in the manor house by volunteer flower arrangers. You will see massive beds of peonies, eucalyptus, zinnias, ageratum, snaps, coneflowers, lisianthus, and sunflowers.

Closer to the house is a superb rose garden enclosed in a perfectly clipped taxus hedge. On the north end of the cutting garden are the working and display greenhouses. Walk from the greenhouses through an arbor to the birch allée, a wonderful 550-foot-long tunnel formed under a canopy of interlacing white bark birches. At one end lies the manor house, a treasure in itself. At the other is a teahouse overlooking the Cuyahoga Valley. From there, rustic stone steps lead down to a water-filled quarry and a marvelous Japanese garden. Wander the trails along the creek and by all means do walk over the steeply arching Japanese bridges that cross and recross the creek. You will eventually come to a shady area, where lies the traditional Japanese garden, which is serene, quiet, secluded. Here you will find offset stone walks and steps (which look like they are the work of nature rather than a careful plan), stone lanterns, gracefully manicured evergreens, trickling water, bamboo, and many other beautiful details.

To the south of this wonderful garden is a naturalistic dell riddled with trails and a sycamore-rhododendron allée that leads back to the manor. The huge sycamores are, unfortunately, stricken with Ceratocystis canker, which is evident in the deterioration of their trunks. Determining how to replace these sycamores without disturbing the rhododendrons is presently being debated, said director John Miller.

On the east side of the manor you will find another garden that has been restored to its original form. This is the blue and gold breakfast garden, Manning's contribution. This small garden lies between brick walks that lead up to a sculpture fountain, a copy of the fifteenth-century Italian, *Boy and Dolphin*. The beds are planted with old-fashioned flowers such as bugleweed, bellflower, morning glory, hosta, squill, violets, iris, narcissus, foxglove, columbine, and lungwort. This garden is just outside the manor's breakfast room and has been restored to resemble an earlier era, from old photos and the recollections of Irene Seiberling Harrison, the last of the Seiberling family who in 1992 was 102 years old.

"The Breakfast Room faced east, so the sun shone through the French doors in the morning. During the summer, Mother would open the doors and open the room out into the garden. We would all look past the doors, and the blue fringe of morning glory that crept up the edge of each, to the sunlit planting and the darling fountain. The drip of water from the fountain added to the serenity of the moment," Harrison said.

If you are not in a rush to get home, drive back along Riverview Road or Akron Peninsula Road through the lovely natural areas of the Cuyahoga Valley National Recreation Area.

Sunnybrook Farms
(9448 Mayfield Rd., Chesterland, 44026; 216-729-7232; guided tours available by advance reservation)

Some of the gardens surrounding Sunnybrook Farms in Chesterland are worth a drive to visit, even if you are not planning to buy anything. When you pull into the nursery at Sunnybrook, you will see a narrow rock garden perched on a high retaining wall beside the greenhouse. In it you will find a nice combination of herbs and alpine plants, a good source of inspiration for your own rock garden. The herb gardens that were maintained west of the driveway in past years, however, are now closed and are likely to remain unattended for some time.

Most fun here is walking down the drive that passes by the garden center area and plastic tunnel greenhouses. Tall evergreen trees and shrubs form a dense wooded area that is honeycombed with narrow paths and is home to epimedium, ferns, and hundreds of different kinds of hostas. The walks crisscross the dark shady garden and meander past interesting woody specimen plants such as variegated pachysandra, *Pieris japonica*, and mammoth taxus shrubs. When you exit the garden, follow the stone lane back toward the greenhouses; it passes a field of sheep, some of whom may come visit you if you call to them.

(See also: Specialty Growers, chapter 3.)

GARDENS OPEN BY APPOINTMENT

The following gardens welcome visitors, but only by prior arrangement with the garden caretakers.

Claystone Farm
(Newbury; open for group tours by appointment only; contact Don Vanderbrook, 371-0164)
This is the working and display garden of nationally known floral designer Don Vanderbrook and his partner Tony Badalamenti. The garden, which stretches across a hillside, has a formal English layout. Main walks run up and down the hill; smaller paths cross perpendicular, creating many rectangular beds between them. Boxwood hedges, clipped hollies, and trellised espalied fruit trees also define areas of the garden.

Masses of flowers ramble across the beds; many are excellent for cutting. Some, such as foxglove, poppies, columbines, and salvias, scatter their seed and pop up where they will, giving a spontaneous look to the otherwise structured garden. Vanderbrook collects flower species and varieties from the Royal Horticultural Society, British flower designers, and other unusual sources, so he often has exotic bloomers on display. Other plants have come from large parties he has decorated; flowering cherries were left after a cherry blossom festival in Washington, D.C.; bamboo remained after it was used to cast shadows on Japanese screens. His most recent garden is devoted to the new shrub roses developed by English breeder David Austin—they have been given much press in horticultural magazines in America.

(See also: Vanderbrook, Don entry in Specialty Growers, chapter 3.)

Gilmour Academy Restored Tudor Garden

(corner of SOM Center and Cedar roads, Gates Mills, 44040; groups welcome with advance reservations; contact development director Jean Buchannan; 473-8001)

Entering the Gilmour campus past brick walls and down a winding road to a historic Tudor house, is a little like entering a different time. But blue tennis courts and groups of jeans-clad students bring you back real fast. Behind the Tudor house is one of the few Warren Manning gardens that remain in Cleveland. (For more on Manning, see the Stan Hywet Hall entry in this chapter). "This is the original house of Francis Drury, a Cleveland industrialist who helped develop the oil stove. It was on Euclid Avenue Mansion Row, where the Drury Theater is now. When the family retired to Gates Mills, Drury had the home reproduced, and moved the garden there, including its original lighting and furnishings," said Jean Buchannan, director of institutional advancement and development.

Actually, not much of the garden remains except the skeleton, but that is due to change, says Buchannan. Gilmour is raising funds for restoration of the home and gardens.

The rectangular sunken garden surrounds a reflecting pool and blends with nearby Tudor architecture, although the massive retaining walls are unsettled at present and in need of major repair. Huge vining hydrangeas climb over the walls, and towering arborvitaes loom in each corner; these are the only original plants remaining. Where flowers used to cluster, pachysandra, sheared taxus, and lawn have taken over. Buchannan envisions returning a greater abundance of flowers as the restoration proceeds. She hopes to use the garden more for school ceremonies, weddings, and other special events, and that perhaps it will again become a living classroom.

"We used to give boys academy appointments—you might have called them detentions—that they spent weeding in the garden. A lot of them ended up learning much about plants and being inspired. One of those boys went on to become the assistant director of The Garden Center," Buchannan said.

Gwinn Estate
(Bratenahl, open by reservation only to nonprofit organizations for meetings, programs, seminars, retreats; for more information contact University Circle Incorporated, 791-3900)

Built in 1907 for William Gwinn Mather, a leading turn-of-the-century industrialist, the Gwinn estate is now used as a conference center. The grounds feature a historical landscape and an elegant home. Unfortunately, it's not open for public visits. But if you get a chance to attend a meeting on the grounds, take it. You will see the work of well-known early landscape architects Charles Platt, Warren Manning, and Ellen Shipman, who collaborated on the property for several decades. The landscape today is not maintained with total historical accuracy, but it retains the original layout, focusing on the wonderful views of Lake Erie and combining natural and formal plantings.

The blending of natural with formal, found in both Gwinn's garden and the Mather home, resulted from using a team of two designers, each of whom proposed a different approach. Charles Platt, an architect and landscape architect, proposed laying out the property using modernized classic Italian designs, which he had written about in *Italian Gardens* (1893, Harper, New York, NY). His influence was felt in the architecture of the home and formal garden, and in the linking of indoor and outdoor spaces. In contrast, Warren Manning enjoyed designing naturalistic gardens, which take up much of the property and enhance the views. He used a large number of native American plants in a style now called "emerging American."

In addition to Manning and Platt, in the late 1930s Ellen Shipman came to Gwinn to create a new planting plan in the existing formal flower gardens. These had been set off from a parklike expanse of lawn and from the lake shoreline by a garden wall and pergola to the north and by a teahouse to the south. As was typical of Shipman gardens, the plan was complex—almost astonishingly so by modern standards—and required high maintenance. Today, her elaborate plans have been simplified but still use the original plant list and color scheme of soft blue and yellow, creamy white, and soft pink. Gwinn gardeners custom-grow many unusual varieties of perennials in the original working greenhouse, which also supplies cut flowers for the house. Fifty years ago, the greenhouse also grew grapes and nectarines for the table.

Roemer Display Garden

*(north of Roemer Nursery, 2310 Green Rd., North Madison, 44057;
428-5178 or 800-955-5178; avail. for tours of 15–30 people by reserv.)*

This one-and-a-half-acre garden is a class act, pretty and
full of unusual plants that will awe a horticultural collector.
You'll walk along winding brick walks and turf paths, which
sometimes widen to show you a broad view over a large section of the garden or narrow so that you look closely at a small
collection of plants nearby. The paths branch out into areas
you can crisscross to find the plants that interest you most.

Interesting plants abound here. You'll see weeping, creeping, and cascading forms, golden hemlocks, and beech trees
with purple leaves edged in pink. There is a water garden,
unusual garden seats—one is made of a big slab of stone—and
such spectacles as a huge old clump of roots that now support
a community of alpine plants.

Carolyn Stroombeek, who devised and now manages the
garden, uses it to test new plants and has found some excep-
tional selections that Roemer Nursery sells wholesale. Most
notable is Schmidt's boxwood, which is exceptionally hardy,
staying healthy despite cold winters that kill other kinds of
boxwood back to the ground.

Further Afield

Here a few special gardens that may require more travel time
for some but are well worth a trip.

Kingwood Center

*(900 Park Ave. West, Mansfield, 44906; 419-522-0211; self-guided
tour brochures available; group tours by advance reservation)*

This spectacular 27-acre garden (with 20 additional acres of woods) is the former estate of C. K. King, once president of Ohio Brass. He left his estate to a trust that now operates Kingwood Center. Because the grounds are free, open dawn to dusk, and full of colorful flowers and impressive formal gardens, Kingwood Center has become a popular park for local residents. It also attracts gardeners from surrounding states who want to see new plants or new planting combinations.

There are massive displays of spring bulbs, including 45,000 tulips and a lawn carpeted with crocuses, a herb garden, formal and informal flower beds, an orangery of unusual indoor plants, and acres of trial gardens for All America Selections (an organization that tests new seed-grown cultivars in gardens across the country and gives awards to outstanding newcomers).

The brilliant—some may say gaudy—swirling annual beds are remarkable. One recent color combination was 'Celebrity Blue' and 'Celebrity Hot Pink' petunias with 'Lavender Lady' globe amaranth and purple *Verbena bonariensis*. Some of the strange and astonishing annuals displayed here have been the swollen, hotdog-shaped crimson flowers of 'Ritz Rocket' amaranth, the tiny plumes of 'Flamingo Feather' cockscomb, tiny, furry tail-like flowers of a miniature chenile plant (*Acalypha repens*), and eight-foot tall purple 'Dwarf Red Spire' castor beans.

"Not many places have as extensive collections as we do that also are put in interesting garden settings. When people want to look at plants, they come to see us because we have just about everything in the better cultivars of peonies, roses, daylilies, iris, and hostas," said Bill Collins, education coordinator.

In the perennial garden are some intriguing and quite unusual specimens, including *Bletilla*, a hardy orchid, bronze-leaf *Ligularia dentata* 'Dark Beauty, and fleece flower (*Polygonum* x 'Border Jewel'). You can find similar "jewels" of the plant world by browsing through the many other garden areas here, which are so extensive and well laid out that you may want to park your car in several different locations around the grounds so you can take it all in during a single afternoon.

Ohio State University Research and Development Center Historic Rose Garden and Secrest Arboretum
(1680 Madison Ave., Wooster, 44691; 263-3700)

This arboretum, named for Edmund Secrest, the first state forester, is a working area where Ohio State University staff and students evaluate new and old plants. You can see magnificent mature specimens of rhododendrons, azaleas, crab apples, hollies, trees, shrubs, and evergreens, including fifty kinds of arborvitae and a hundred kinds of taxus. Some of these were planted as long ago as 1909. You'll also see:

The Garden of Roses of Legend and Romance
Of special interest to lovers of historic roses, this garden is in peak bloom in June. This two-and-a-half-acre garden includes about five hundred varieties of roses of antiquity, legend, and romance, including old moss, species, damask, eglanteria, scotch, cabbage, alba, foetida, bourbon, gallica roses along with old climbers, ramblers, and other roses.

Agricultural Technical Institute's Horticultural Gardens
The nearby ATI Horticultural Gardens (1328 Dover Rd., Wooster, 44691; 264-3911) feature gardens of herbs, perennials, English roses, espalied pyracantha, perennials, a greenhouse-conservatory, and an All America Display Garden of annuals.

Quailcrest Farm

(2810 Armstrong Rd., Wooster, 44691; 345-6722)

This wonderful nursery garden is small in comparison to its neighbor, Kingwood Center, but it is well maintained, comfortable, and full of good ideas and interesting plants. Thirty-five display and trial gardens surround the house, and there are nursery areas set within the beautiful velvety-green lawn. Discover an unusual toad lily in a shade garden, a passion flower vining on an arbor in the herb garden, and curly-leaved parsley used as a frilly edging for a mixed shrub and flower garden. Several color combinations are particularly striking in fall, a time many other gardens are failing: a drift of 'Purple Palace' coralbells nestled in front of crimson-flowered sedum 'Autumn Joy', and, in another garden, crimson snapdragons at the feet of the red berries of a cranberry viburnum bush.

(See also: Special Events, chapter 2; Specialty Growers, chapter 3.)

Otto Schoepfle Arboretum

(11106 Market St., Birmingham,; 800-526-7275; staffed 8 a.m. to 4 p.m. weekdays; tours avail. with advance reservation)

This arboretum, one of Lorain County's best-kept secrets, is the home of Otto Schoepfle, former chairman of the board of the *Elyria Chronicle Telegram* and current garden columnist. He has developed 22 acres of gardens adjoining 50 acres of woods and meadows along the Vermilion River. Schoepfle has donated the arboretum to the Lorain County Metroparks, which now helps maintain the gardens.

The arboretum is formally designed in the front, then changes to naturalistic plantings and, ultimately, to native woodlots. It features clipped hedges, unusual beech trees, a harem of mature American hollies (one male with 15 females), perennial borders, a pine grove with rhododendrons, and astilbe and hosta collections.

"There is a European influence, which Mr. Schoepfle brought back from his travels. And there is something of interest at all times, including winter, when you can see the shedding bark of stewartia, the bright colors of red twig dogwood, the curving stems of contorted filberts, and the evergreen topiary," said Joel Loufman, horticulturist. Fortunately, most everything is labeled so you can learn while you wander.

Zoar Village
(State Rte. 212, 3 mi. off Interstate 77, Zoar)

Zoar Village was founded in the 1800s by a cult of religious separatists. They built their cabins, started subsistence farming, then created a two-acre garden in the center of town. They surrounded a central planting of trees and shrubs with circular beds of flowers, an impressive sight today and certainly a phenomenon in pioneer times. Beside the garden is one of the first greenhouses in Ohio, which was used to house houseplants of wealthy Clevelanders during the winter.

Unfortunately, the future of the 18-acre Zoar Village State Memorial is uncertain because of Ohio Historical Society budget cuts.

ATRIUMS AND INDOOR PLANTINGS

When the weather becomes too hot or cold to enjoy outdoor gardens, you might try browsing through some of the local atriums. Many of the larger and newer office buildings include an area of skylights and greenery, often accompanied by water. Malls, too, often have plenty of greenery and can be wonderful places to walk for exercise and to experience a touch of the tropics in the winter. Many of the mall owners compete to put up the most lavish indoor plant displays—and you can be the beneficiary even if you don't buy a thing. The pace tends to pick up closer to Christmas, says Mary Blaha from Interior Green, an interior plantscaping company, as many offices and malls call in their plantscapers to add flowering plants, Christmas trees (though most are silk), and other festive decorations. Here are a few enjoyable atriums in town:

BP America Building *(Public Square)*
This large atrium area has warm and quiet landscaping that features a few large trees and a fountain.

The Arcade *(401 Euclid Ave.)*
Simple vines soften this busy five-story arcade with high glass ceiling. It's not a horticultural showplace, but the window boxes of green vines (which include durable grape ivy) stand out amid the shopping bustle. The Arcade puts on an especially ornate Christmas greens display.

Tower City Center *(Public Square)*
Plantings are not the dominant factor here; fountains, towering glass ceilings, and endless balconies of shops are. But take a closer look at the cast-iron plants, such as Chinese evergreens, which look good even though they grow on the balconies, where light levels are quite low.

AREAS TO DRIVE THROUGH

The following are not gardens but attractive growing areas to drive through and view from your car:

Exceptional Cleveland Street Trees

When you are in Cleveland, you may want to drive through some of the streets lined with especially interesting trees—a few of which are cultivars found or developed here in Cleveland. Some of these are:

• Callery pears along Ferndale Avenue, where the cultivar 'Cleveland Select' was originally discovered. 'Cleveland Select' trees also line West 172nd Street south of Puritas.

• Norway maples on Parkhurst Drive, where the cultivar 'Cleveland' was discovered. 'Cleveland' Norway maples line Brooklawn Avenue.

• 'Bowhall' maples stretch along Mayview Road.

• 'Briotii' hybrid horse chestnuts bloom bright red on West 58th Street.

• Korean evodia along Cortland Dr. off West 140th Street.

• Japanese tree lilacs produce fragrant white flowers in late June and early July on Fairville Avenue off Rocky River Drive.

Avon Greenhouse District

You can find a number of nurseries and greenhouses around Avon. From Detroit Road, travel south on Stony Ridge.

Lake County Nurseries and Greenhouses

(State Routes 20 and 84, and nearby areas from Heisley Rd. to Madison in Lake County)

Despite a gradual decline in the number of growers, you will still find many nurseries, greenhouses, and garden centers clustered in this part of Lake County. If you are looking for new plants, you can find just about anything along this route. The fertile soils and mild lake-effect weather here is perfect for nursery crops, orchards, and grapes, which you will find in abundance. This area once was called the Nursery Capital of the United States, a title now shared by warmer areas like Florida and California.

Schaaf Road / Brooklyn Greenhouse District

This area of fertile sandy soils once housed market gardens and was later a center for a thriving greenhouse industry. Although most of the greenhouse ranges have given way to industry and housing, you can still see an impressive collection of ranges, many of which are wholesale only. Drop in on the few businesses that welcome retail customers. Look for Richardson's Greenhouse, Rosby Brothers, and, on nearby Jennings Road, Christensen Greenhouse.

West Shoreway in Cleveland
(off West Shoreway by W. 49th St. exit)

What was recently a nine-acre dumping place for old concrete, kitchen sinks, and granite blocks has become a meadow of little bluestem, blazing-star, and black-eyed Susan. And, by 1995, Cleveland landscape architect Judith Vargo expects the land to have matured into a prairie of ten species. "This is the first time the city has done this kind of prairie planting instead of planting turf grass (which gets boring after a while). We liked the idea that the prairie is intended to be self-maintaining," said Vargo.

CHAPTER TWO

~

Gardening Education, Information, and Events

MAYBE YOU MADE A FEW MISTAKES in your early gardening efforts and now want to rework them. Or perhaps you find yourself redesigning your gardens or landscapes as your tastes and needs change over time. Because there are so many different plants that can be grown (34,000 are listed in *Hortus III*, a dictionary of cultivated plants) and at least as many combinations of microclimates, soil variations, and uses for vegetation, the gardening field offers limitless possibilities. You could garden, read, and study your entire life and never learn everything there is to know about growing plants. Though you certainly can get a good idea of how to plant and tend your own yard, gardening is an art you can continue to learn and grow with in every passing year.

Gardeners have different needs and interests, and those needs and interests can change with time. A young couple with children and a small suburban lot may want to keep their landscaping simple. But later on, if they find themselves with more space and time, they might want to begin perennial gardening or try raising their own vegetables. Perhaps this couple will need a break from the pressures of work and will decide to make their yard into a hidden retreat with a patio, waterfall, and waterlily pool. Someone who has given up house and yard for a condominium might spend time once reserved for mowing the lawn on growing bonsai on the patio or tending an indoor light garden full of orchids. Another person, tired of working behind a desk or counter, may decide to return to school and become a landscape architect or tackle a certificate program to become a nurseryman.

The bottom line is, each of us can keep learning. You can let your yard evolve to reflect your own lifestyle or let the way you earn a living reflect the kind of life you want to live. Learn so you can try something new. Learn so you can do any job right the first time. As you will see in the following educational listing, you are not limited by educational opportunities and should never suffer from lack of available gardening knowledge.

You can choose among all-encompassing, formal college programs or shorter, more focused community, garden center, or arboretum classes. Mix pleasure with learning by visiting horticultural festivals or taking garden tours. Pick up the phone and call one of several horticultural hotlines to resolve a specific garden problem. Or simply select a good book at a nearby library to find your answers in peace and solitude.

Adult Education

Organized by Less-Formal, Intermediate, and Formal programs; listed alphabetically by sponsoring organization.

Less-Formal Programs

Community Education Programs
Many local community education programs offer gardening, landscaping, or flower-arranging classes, especially dur-

ing the spring. Contact your local school system, recreation board, or community center for information. If your community does not offer a topic that interests you, check with neighboring communities.

The Garden Center of Greater Cleveland
(11030 East Blvd., Cleveland, 44106; 721-1600)

Besides holding many plant shows and seasonal extravaganzas, The Garden Center offers short classes and more extensive symposiums on a variety of horticultural subjects. Recent programs at the Center included guest speaker Dr. Alex Shigo, the plant pathologist who has revolutionized pruning techniques, and a special three-day seminar of experts speaking on the historical preservation of landscapes. The Garden Center co-sponsors lectures with many of the local plant societies, so both groups can benefit from the expertise of national authorities. Garden Center staff and instructors also hold short (one- to several-session) classes in landscape design, flower arranging, and gardening.

(See also Intermediate Programs in this section, Children's Gardening Programs, Horticultural Therapy, Garden Libraries, and Special Events in this chapter; Gardens Open to the Public, chapter 1; Specialty Growers, chapter 3; General Horticultural Organizations, chapter 4.)

Great Lakes Herb Symposium
(contact Jamie Barrow: P.O Box 402, Hiram, 44234-0402)

A three-day symposium with programs, tours, and top speakers in the field of herbs comes every few years to the Hiram College Campus. It was held here most recently in 1992 and so may not return for a few years, but watch for it because it is well worth attending. Past themes have focused on herbal cuisine, fragrant herbs, and garden design in medieval and Victorian times.

Holden Arboretum
(9500 Sperry Rd., Kirtland, 44060; 946-4400)

Holden sponsors short (one- to several-session) programs that are nature- and gardening-oriented. Holden staff and a few outside experts teach about native and cultivated plants (as well as wildlife such as bald eagles, marsh wrens, and black terns). In the classroom, they get down to complicated topics like plant taxonomy and the use of plant keys, or practical issues like landscaping, planting window baskets or using herbs.

(See also: Intermediate Programs in this section; Children's Gardening Programs, Horticultural Therapy, Garden Libraries, and Special Events in this chapter; Gardens Open to the Public, chapter 1; Specialty Growers, chapter 3; General Horticultural Organizations, chapter 4.)

Ivy Tree Bed and Breakfast
(195 S. Professor St., Oberlin, 44074; 774-4510 after 5:30 p.m.)

This Oberlin bed-and-breakfast features occasional weekend workshops given by Steve Coughlin, landscape designer for Barnes' Nursery in Huron. The late 1800s Colonial Revival and Victorian home features a garden that Coughlin is developing. Call for information about his occasional Garden Gathering Weekends, featuring lectures, tours, and the company of other gardeners.

Lake County Farmpark
(8800 Chardon Rd., Kirtland, 44094; 800-366-3276)

Take a regularly scheduled tour to learn how the park has re-created gardens of history. Or enjoy special events that will show how gardens and farms were handled in bygone years.

(See also: Gardens Open to the Public, chapter 1.)

Lake View Cemetery
(12316 Euclid Ave., Cleveland, 44106-4393; 421-2665)
During the spring and early summer blooming season, Lake View offers occasional guided walks that teach about the unusual plants at this cemetery. Call for information. (See also: Gardens Open to the Public, chapter 1.)

Lakeland Community College
(7700 Clocktower Dr., Mentor, 44060-7594; contact: Nursery Production Coordinator: 953-7213; Community Education: 953-7116)
Lakeland Community College offers one- to six-session community education programs in perennial gardening, herb gardening, home landscaping, floral design, and the art of bonsai. (See also: Formal Programs in this section.)

North Coast Pruning
(P.O. Box 0428, Oberlin, 44070; 774-1556)
North Coast Pruning owner, Mark Long, specializes in teaching people how to prune properly. He offers educational programs for garden clubs and other groups, training sessions for grounds crews, pruning workshops, and one-on-one instruction for homeowners.

Sea World
(1100 Sea World Dr., Aurora, 44202; Head Horticulturist: 995-2156; Tour Booking: 995-2152)
Sea World staff horticulturists occasionally hold gardening lectures and tours of their grounds. They also are available to give group tours that emphasize a variety of subjects and then let you enjoy the other pleasures of the park at discounted admission rates. (See also: Gardens Open to the Public, chapter 1.)

Sunnybrook Farms
(9448 Mayfield Rd., Chesterland, 44026; 729-7232)

Tim Ruh, owner of Sunnybrook Farms, sometimes invites nationally known landscape designers, book authors, garden experts, and herb crafters to speak at nursery festivals or day-long symposiums at the Cleveland Museum of Natural History. Call the nursery to see what he has in store during the growing season and ask to be placed on their mailing list.

(See also: Gardens Open to the Public, chapter 1; Specialty Growers, chapter 3.)

Intermediate Programs

The Garden Center of Greater Cleveland
(11030 East Blvd., Cleveland, 44106; 721-1600)

In addition to their less-formal educational offerings, The Garden Center also has a horticulture certificate program, which includes such classes as botany, plant identification, pruning, bed preparation, and plant selection. Participants must take a total of 12 core classes and three electives within a one- to three-year period.

(See also Intermediate Programs in this section; Children's Gardening Programs, Horticultural Therapy, Garden Libraries, and Special Events in this chapter.)

Holden Arboretum
(9500 Sperry Rd., Kirtland, 44060; 946-4400)

Holden offers a landscape certificate program that awards certification after attendance at 12 core classes and other electives in plant science, plant materials, and design.

(See also Intermediate Programs in this section; Children's Gardening Programs, Horticultural Therapy, Garden Libraries, and Special Events in this chapter.)

Master Gardener Program
(Varied locations; organized by the Ohio Cooperative Extension Service of Ohio State University; County offices: Cuyahoga: 631-1890, Geauga: 834-4656, Lake: 357-2582, Lorain: 322-0127, Medina: 725-4911, Summit: 497-1611)
Residents can train with their County Extension Service to be Master Gardeners and aquire the basics of most aspects of horticulture. The classes, held between January and April (actual dates change every year) include eight full-day sessions held on Wednesdays. They are taught by Extension professionals, university professors, and specialists. On finishing the course, Master Gardeners must complete 50 hours of volunteer work in gardening fields. The class is limited to about thirty people per year, so sign up early. Material costs run about $50.

Formal Programs

Agricultural Technical Institute
(1328 Dover Rd., Wooster, 44691-9989; 264-3911 or 800-647-8283)
The Wooster-based Agricultural Technical Institute of Ohio State University offers two-year associate of applied sciences degrees in floral design and marketing, greenhouse production and management, grounds management, landscape construction and contracting, nursery and garden center management, and turf-grass management. Programs in agriculture and animal industries are also offered.

Horticulture students take general college courses in science, math, communications, and social science. The remaining 60 percent of their studies are concentrated on courses in their chosen field that include hands-on experience in campus greenhouses, outdoor display gardens, and floral shops, as well as an internship.

Cleveland State University

(CSU Department of Community Education; Applied Technologies; 2344 Euclid Ave., Room 103, Cleveland, 44105; 687-4850)

The CSU Department of Continuing Education offers a popular two-year certificate program in landscape/horticulture. There are six required classes, held one evening a week for eight weeks. They include introductory horticulture and landscape operations, turf grasses, integrated pest-management, landscape design, trees and shrubs, and flowers. They also have other short courses on specialities such as landscape construction and landscape lighting.

Cuyahoga Community College

(Plant Science Program, Eastern Campus, 4250 Richmond Rd., Highland Heights, 44122; 987-2035)

This new program is the first four-year plant science technology degree offered in the Cleveland area. It has been developed to train skilled personnel to work in greenhouses, florist shops, landscaping, landscape architecture, nurseries, golf-course turf maintenance, and horticultural sales.

Cuyahoga Community College also offers a two-year associate of applied science degree combining classroom, laboratory, and field studies in soils, plant pathology, plant production, identification, landscape design, general contracting, retail floriculture, and related business and social sciences.

Kent State University

(Department of Biological Sciences, 256 Cunningham Hall, Kent State University, Kent, 44242; 672-2444)

Kent offers a degree in biology and college-level classes in plant anatomy, systematic botany, morphology of lower plants, local flora, genetics, plant physiology, and organic evolution—any of which might be of interest to serious students of horticulture or nature.

Lakeland Community College

(7700 Clocktower Dr., Mentor, 44060-7594; contact Nursery Production Coordinator: 953-7213; Community Education: 953-7116; see also Informal Programs in this section)

Lakeland Community College offers a two-year certificate in nursery production, which is geared toward developing supervisors or middle-management staff for nurseries. It requires students to take 17 five-session courses in plant science, supervisory management, effective communication, pest management, plant nutrition, water management, nursery equipment, maintenance, and operation, plus six months of field experience in a horticulture work site.

Ohio State University

(College of Agriculture, 100 Agricultural Administration Building, 2120 Fyffe Rd., Columbus, 43210; 614-292-1589;
• *Dept. of Urban Forestry, School of Natural Resources: 379 Kottman Hall, 2021 Coffey Rd., Columbus, 43210; 614-292-2265;*
• *Dept. of Landscape/Horticulture: 152 Howlett Hall, 2001 Fyffe Ct., Columbus, 43210-1007; 614-292-0281)*

The horticultural college for the state of Ohio is well respected but has recently suffered from budget cuts. Students can earn four-year bachelor degrees and advanced degrees in horticulture and related areas. In the landscape/horticulture program alone, students can specialize in commercial landscaping, production and sales, fruit crops, or vegetable crops. Graduates work in jobs in a variety of fields, including greenhouse management, landscape design, horticultural sales or teaching, interior plantscaping, nursery or farm management, or pest management.

Vocational Schools

High-school students interested in a career in horticulture can get a head start by attending their district's vocational school. In the evenings, most of these facilities also offer continuing education for adults.

Cuyahoga Valley Joint Vocational School

(8001 Brecksville Rd., Brecksville, 44141-1294; 526-5200)

This large vocational school serves communities to the south of Cleveland, including school systems in Brecksville-Broadview Heights, Cuyahoga Heights, Garfield Heights, Independence, Nordonia Hills, North Royalton, Revere, and Twinsburg. It has an extensive adult education listing; over 16,000 adults attended these classes during the 1991-92 school year.

In addition, there is a two-year horticulture program for high school juniors and seniors; it's also offered tuition-free to adult residents or employees of businesses in the affiliated school districts. The horticulture program consists of eight nine-week classes—540 hours of instruction per year.

Mayfield Vocational Horticulture School

(Gates Mills Horticultural Center, 390 County Line Rd., Gates Mills, 44040; 423-4631; open houses: December sale of holiday decorations and May sale of annuals, perennials, and vegetables)

High-school students from Mayfield, Aurora, Beachwood, Chagrin Falls, Orange, Richmond Heights, Solon, West Geauga, Bedford, and Cleveland Heights can take a half-day junior- and senior-year program at the horticultural center. Instructors teach classes in landscape design, construction and maintenance, greenhouse and garden center management, floral design and crops, turf- and golf-course management, nursery stock, and small-engine maintenance. Students also can co-op, working in a horticulture-related job two days a week, and attending the center three days a week.

Mentor Vocational Program
(6477 Center St., Mentor, 44060; 255-4444 ext. 370.)
The horticultural vocational program at Mentor High School (available to students in the Euclid, Brush, Willoughby South, Eastlake North, and Wickliffe school systems) taps the wealth of nurseries and landscaping operations in Lake County to enrich the students' education. It also stands apart from other programs because up to 60 percent of the graduating class go on to two- or four-year college programs in horticulture. "Kids need a competitive advantage to be successful in today's society and we bend over backwards to give it to them," said Karl Hagedorn, horticulture instructor.

The curriculum includes an introduction to horticulture for tenth grade Mentor students. Juniors from all the participating Lakeshore schools can attend three hours of daily laboratory and classroom learning in floriculture, landscape-turf, plant identification, plant and soil science, and equipment operation. Seniors combine classes that touch on business and management, with three hours of daily on-the-job experience.

Polaris Career Center
(7285 Old Oak Blvd., Middleburg Hts., 44130; 243-8600
Juniors and seniors from Berea, Strongsville, North Olmsted, Olmsted Falls, and Fairview Park can spend half the day in horticultural vocational training and the other half at their home school. Juniors take a comprehensive overview of floral

design, landscaping, greenhouse and nursery production, and turf maintenance, then go on to take a summer job in the field. Those students who maintain an *A* average for 95 percent of their classes can continue working in horticulture as part of their senior year laboratory. Other students are placed in internships for the last nine weeks of the school year.

"We have a special advantage here because every kind of horticultural industry is within driving distance—large nurseries, wholesale houses—you name it, we have it. It's a great opportunity for the kids," said Tom Evans, horticulture instructor.

Washington Park Horticulture Center

(3875 Washington Park Blvd., Cleveland, 44105;
high school program: 441-8070; adult education: 441-8075)

This horticulture center, operated by the Cleveland public schools, has the largest public school greenhouse in the state of Ohio plus 57 acres of park land with an arboretum and sports fields. These facilities house a high-school vocational program that emphasizes landscaping involving sports turf and equipment—a program that is undergoing restructuring. Classes are offered in landscape and sports turf, landscape mechanics, small animal care, floral design, and interior plantscaping.

Washington Park also offers adult vocational programs for residents of northeast Ohio; it's the largest adult vocational agribusiness program of its kind in the state. The staple among these offerings is a commercial floral design certificate program that consists of 96 hours of hands-on classroom instruction. Classes in recreational flower arranging and day-long floral workshops on special holiday themes and interior plant identification and care are also offered. Periodically, the Center gives classes in gardening, mechanics and small-engine repair, and beginning and advanced bonsai.

West Technical High School

(2201 W. 93rd St., Cleveland, 44102; 634-2215)

The vocational program at West Tech serves the Cleveland School System but offers a different program from Washington Park. The two-year horticulture/floriculture program for juniors and seniors emphasizes landscape design and construction. Students learn to use fertilizers, landscape tools, and equipment; they study garden center management and floral design; they learn skills of plant production, propagation, maintenance, and sales; they also study plant identification and soil science.

Another two-year program concentrates on landscape design and construction, teaching identification and use of landscape plants, landscape design, estimating, and installation.

A one-year program is devoted to greenhouse production/management and sales, teaching high school students to grow and market plants.

High-school freshmen and sophomores can take a one-year course in diversified agriculture, an overview of plant identification, small animal care, and landscape design.

Children's Gardening Programs

The Garden Center of Greater Cleveland

(11030 East Blvd., Cleveland, 44106; 721-1600)

The Garden Center offers its own programs for kids, including seasonal library story times and fun classes that feature planting or crafts focused around a plant or holiday theme.

School or church classes, Scout troops, and similar groups

with fewer than 35 children can arrange classes or tours with children's specialists at The Garden Center.

Green Thumb Club
(contact The Garden Center of Greater Cleveland, 721-1600)

School kids throughout greater Cleveland can buy inexpensive flower and vegetable seeds, fertilizer, and gardening instructions through the Green Thumb Club, a program jointly sponsored by The Garden Center, the Cleveland Public Schools, and the *Plain Dealer*. At the end of the growing season, kids are rewarded for their gardening effort with certificates, buttons, pins, ribbons, and free admission to the Cuyahoga County Fair.

Green Thumb groups must have five or more children and be sponsored by an adult or group of adults who can pick up supplies, supervise the gardens, and organize a garden fair or fall display.

Holden Arboretum
(9500 Sperry Rd., Kirtland, 44060; 946-4400)

Holden offers an extensive children's program, including such classes as Insects Through a Toddler's Eyes (ages 2 and 3 with adult) and Monster Rock Walk (ages 7 to 10).

Indoor School Garden Program
(contact The Garden Center of Greater Cleveland, 721-1600)

With the aid of a GrowLab light garden, elementary schoolchildren can grow plants indoors year-round in their classrooms. The kids think it's fun; teachers use it as a laboratory of hands-on activities to accompany science, math, art, and other curriculums. The program, which began in 1986, has placed over 45 GrowLabs in Cleveland Public School classrooms.

Lake County Farmpark
(8800 Chardon Rd., Kirtland, 44094; 800-366-FARM)

Lake County Farmpark offers educational tours for school classes and other children's groups.

Lake Erie Nature and Science Center
(28728 Wolf Rd., Bay Village, 44140; 871-2900)

Kids can learn about nature and science during daytime preschool classes, after-school programs for schoolchildren, and through hikes, field studies, and classroom observations at the Lake Erie Nature and Science Center. The Nature and Science Center also offers programs for children's groups.

Shaker Lakes Regional Nature Center
(2600 South Park Blvd., Shaker Heights, 44120; 321-5935)

Kids from ages 2 to 9, and sometimes 10- and 11-year-olds, can participate in environmentally oriented programs, including plant identification and seed growing, held once a week during the school season or daily during the summer. The Nature Center also offers programs for children's groups.

HORTICULTURAL THERAPY

Two area programs, sponsored by The Garden Center and Holden Arboretum, use plants to help young, old, disabled, and disadvantaged people feel better about themselves and develop physically, intellectually, and socially. The programs are run by trained horticultural therapists who tailor horticultural programs to meet the needs of many different kinds of people.

Horticultural therapy has been around in many forms for a very long time. For ages, people have used gardens and gardening for quiet pleasure, introspection, and contentment as well as fresh air and exercise. It is reported that even early Egyptian doctors prescribed a stroll through the garden for disturbed patients. More recently, horticultural therapy has been formalized in treatment programs, and now it is even possible to obtain a degree in horticultural therapy from many universities.

The Garden Center of Greater Cleveland
(11030 East Blvd., Cleveland, 44106; 721-1600)

At The Garden Center, two part-time horticultural therapists consult with health and human service agencies to help develop new programs. They conduct 10-session spring and fall workshops for the Golden Age Centers of Greater Cleveland and offer seasonal workshops at The Garden Center and at selected institutions, including the Sight Center, Camp Cheerful, Health Hill, Eliza Jennings Home, Rainbow Babies and Childrens Hospital, and many others.

Holden Arboretum
(9500 Sperry Rd., Kirtland, 44060; 946-4400)

At Holden, a single, full-time horticultural therapist concentrates on training therapists at certain nursing homes or rehabilitation centers. "I customize my programs to fit into their existing treatment programs. They learn to use horticulture as a motivational and rehabilitation program within the existing institution," said Karen Haas. To a lesser extent, she may work directly with patients at a particular institution on a regular basis over an extended period of time.

GARDEN LIBRARIES

Gardening is popular among readers, and reading is popular among gardeners. Consequently, you can find many gardening resources at area lending or reference libraries. In addition to popular books, many libraries also have gardening magazines, videos, and, in certain cases, catalogs and antique books.

Cleveland Museum of Natural History Library
(Wade Oval, Cleveland, 44106; 231-4600)
This noncirculating library has a large collection of botanical and native plant magazines, journals, and books. They also have a few books on gardening with native plants.

Cleveland Public Library
(Main Branch, 325 Superior Ave., Cleveland, 44114; 623-2800; see the phone book for branch libraries)
For gardeners, the Cleveland Public Library has a large collection of gardening books, including 62 gardening dictionaries, 32 books of garden fiction, and 44 books on the gardens of England, many of which were written in the late 1800s and early 1900s. In the special collections section, you can see herbals, culinary guides, and botanical prints collected since 1869. Go back even further in time by looking at the older herbals and journals in the rare book section (which are not available for borrowing). You'll find modern gardening books in the science and technology section of the library.

Cuyahoga County Public Library
(see the phone book for a complete listing of branches)
Among the many branches of the Cuyahoga County Public Library system you can find most of the better gardening books and magazines. If your local branch doesn't have what you need, you can have books or magazines sent from other branches.

The Garden Center of Greater Cleveland
Eleanor Squire Library
(11030 East Blvd., Cleveland, 44016; 721-1600)
This 15,000-volume library of gardening, landscape architecture, flower arranging, children's, and teaching books is one of the largest of its kind in the country. Books circulate to members for three weeks at a time; nonmembers may use the books for reference in the library. There are 200 different garden-oriented magazines and 750 rare historical books (accessible by appointment). You can find over a thousand nursery and garden supply catalogs, over a hundred videos, and a file of speakers who can talk to groups on horticultural and related subjects. The library also publishes a newsletter, *Off the Shelf.*

Gardenview Horticultural Park Library
(16711 Pearl Rd., Rte. 42, Strongsville, 44136; by appointment only; 238-6653)
This strictly reference library is open to Gardenview members by appointment. It contains over four thousand volumes, especially British classics and monographs on special items, including roses, primroses, magnolias, rhododendrons, and azaleas. Most are for advanced gardeners.
(See also: Gardens Open to the Public, chapter 1.)

Herb Society of America

(9019 Kirtland-Chardon Rd., Mentor 44060; 256-0514; call for open hours)

This is the national headquarters of the Herb Society of America, where a small staff keeps a library of about six hundred herb-related books. The library is open for reference only, and available for use only with HSA staff supervision.

Holden Arboretum

(9500 Sperry Rd., Kirtland, 44060; 946-4400; admission fee for nonmembers; closed Mondays)

The Arboretum library, open for reference only, holds about 6,300 horticulture-related books. It also has 1,200 volumes of rare books that are available for research by appointment only. You will also find 125 magazines, vertical files, a collection of color slides, and three videos—"A Flying Piece of the Sky" (about bluebirds), "In Wonder of Trees," and "The Sugar Bush"—that can be leased by schools or community groups.

GARDENING PUBLICATIONS

If you are focusing on one particular kind of plant and have trouble finding books that are detailed enough at a library, check with a plant society in that field. Some have small libraries that their members may use; others can refer you to their favorite publications. You also may want to subscribe to a magazine on the subject; many provide month after month of ideas and inspiration. If you want to browse a bit yourself, write for catalogs or subscription information from gardening publishers. Some of the better ones are:

Books
- Goosefoot Acres Press, P.O. Box 18016, Cleveland Hts., 44118; 932-2145; books by local author Peter Gail on edible weeds and Amish lifestyles
- Rodale Press, 33 E. Minor Street, Emmaus, PA 18098
- Storey Communications, Schoolhouse Road, Pownal, VT 05261
- Timber Press, 9999 S.W. Wilshire, Suite 124, Portland, OR 97225-9962

Magazines
- *Fine Gardening*, P.O. Box 355, Newtown, CT 06470
- *Flower and Garden*, 4251 Pennsylvania Avenue, Kansas City, MO 64111
- *Horticulture*, 98 N. Washington Street, Boston, MA 02114
- *National Gardening*, 180 Flynn Avenue, Burlington, VT 05401
- *Organic Gardening*, 33 E. Minor Street, Emmaus, PA 18098

Other Periodicals
- *North Coast Garden*, Alan Hirt's consumer guide to gardening; P.O. Box 351, Valley City, 44280; $17 for 10 issues per year.
- *Ohio Gardening*, Cuyahoga County Cooperative Extension Service, 3200 W 65th Street, Cleveland, 44102; 631-1890.
- Many clubs, plant societies, and professional groups have regular newsletters. (See individual listings in chapter 4.)

OTHER ANSWER SOURCES

Sometimes answers to specific questions are as close as your telephone. If you can get through to the experts answering these popular telephone hotlines and newspaper columns, you may find a free solution.

Cooperative Extension Services
(Ohio Cooperative Extension Service, Ohio State University)
Cuyahoga County: 631-1890
Master Gardeners answer gardening questions from 9 a.m. to noon Monday and Tuesdays, and from 1 to 4 p.m. on Thursdays. Questions on preserving fruits and vegetables are answered 1 to 4 p.m. on Tuesday and Fridays.
For prerecorded seasonal gardening tips, call the Home and Garden Teletip (631-1895) or AnswerLine (631-7760).

Other County Extension Services set different schedules for answering questions. Call them for more information:

Geauga: 834-4656
Lake: 357-2582
Lorain: 322-0127
Medina: 725-4911
Summit: 497-1611

The Garden Center of Greater Cleveland
(Gardening Information: 721-0400)
Staff horticulturists answer garden questions 9 a.m. to noon and 1 to 4 p.m. Tuesday and Thursday, and 1 to 4 p.m. Saturdays.

Ohio State University Cooperative Extension Service Plant and Pest Diagnostic Clinic
(OSU, 110 Kottman Hall, 2021 Coffey Rd., Columbus, 43210; 614-292-5006)

Pest and disease diagnostic services are available for a $5 fee if sent through the local Cooperative Extension Service; $12 if you send it yourself. Hard-to-identify plant viruses cost an additional $15 to $50.

Ohio State University Research Extension Analytical Laboratory
(1680 Madison Ave., Wooster, 44691; 263-3760)

Soil sample analysis: obtain test kits from local County Extension Service office.

The Plain Dealer
(1801 Superior Ave., Cleveland, 44114)

Some questions submitted in writing are answered by Jack Kerrigan, county extension agent, in a regular Saturday column.

Sun Newspapers
(5510 Cloverleaf Rd., Cleveland, 44125)

Some questions submitted in writing are answered in "The Green Scene" column.

Special Events:
Festivals, Fairs, and Shows

You can have fun, find unique plants or crafts, and learn a little by attending some of the special events put on by garden centers, clubs, nurseries, and rural community organizations. The list of special events that follows is by no means comprehensive; it only includes some of best-attended or most regular events. There are many other festivals that you will discover if you watch ads and entertainment previews in the local newspapers, especially during the growing season.

To profit the most from special events, take a little time to look closely at the booths, crafts, and plants. Read the labels on plants and jot down the cultivar names of the ones you like. Note how a craftsman has braided lavender stalks together, made a cornhusk doll out of an ear of field corn, or turned apples into fritters. These are all things you can do yourself, if you are provided with a few tips from the artisan whose work you are admiring or if you are willing to read a book on the subject.

Cleveland Home and Flower Show
(Cleveland Convention Center; late February or early March; entry fee; 621-3145)

Retired *Plain Dealer* garden editor Irma Bartell Dugan handles the gardening displays for the Home and Flower Show. She continues to make them more interesting, and she attracts top area landscapers and growers to participate. "We always give the public the first breath and scent of spring and try to give people a lot of take-home ideas with the display gardens along with the latest in home accessories. It is a solid show of gardens and comprehensive approach to a person's surroundings and how to improve them," Dugan said.

The Garden Center of Greater Cleveland: Spring and Christmas Shows

(11030 East Blvd., Cleveland, 44106; held in March or April and December, respectively; free admittance; 721-1600)

As a preview to spring and the winter holidays, The Garden Center fills its halls with plants, both traditional and unusual, plus flower arrangements, collectibles, and props—towns, ponds, woods—whatever will depict the theme for the year. The work is done, in large part, by a volunteer committee with a staff coordinator. "We want to bring families to The Garden Center and provide seasonal activities that are both educational and enjoyable," said director Alexander Apanius. "People can enjoy the spirit of the season and get ideas for their own holidays or gardens. They can learn more about plants and how to take care of them, especially if they attend some of the classes we offer during the shows."

Huntsburg Pumpkin Festival

(15 mi. east of Chester Township; held one weekend in early Oct.)

This annual pumpkin festival features pumpkin baked goods, a pumpkin show, totem poles of pumpkins, squash and gourds, carved pumpkins, pumpkin pottery, old-fashioned games, pony rides, entertainment, and a Fun Run.

Lake County Farmpark

(8800 Chardon Rd., Kirtland, 44094; 1-800-366-3276)

Special events at Lake County Farmpark include Threshing Days in July, Bud Day in September, a Fall Harvest in September, and Cornucopia (about corn) in October.

(See also: Gardens Open to the Public, chapter 1.)

National Home and Garden Show
(IX Center; early March; entry fee; contact Stern Advertising, 464-4850)

Like the Cleveland Home and Flower Show, the National Home and Garden Show features display gardens, some of which are put in by show staff, others by area landscapers and nurseries. The producers often tie one garden into an event put on by Cleveland arts or theater groups, bringing to life gardens from books and operas. Another highlight is the Boulevard of Dreams, a street of several fully landscaped homes, plus a home improvement section, lawn and garden retail area, and arts and crafts booths. The show is easily accessible to wheelchairs.

"The public comes here to look for gardening and landscaping ideas and to see what's available and popular. We usually have landscapers man the displays and if you talk to them you can get a lot of good information," said Rob Attwell, one of the show producers.

Quailcrest Fall Herb Fair
(2810 Armstrong Rd., Wooster, 44691; first Sunday after Labor Day; 345-6722)

Quailcrest Farm brings in 60 gift and art exhibitors, music, and food for a day-long festival in the country.

(See also: Further Afield, chapter 1; Specialty Growers, chapter 3.)

Richardson's Greenhouse and Farm Market Fall Festival
(375 Tuxedo Ave., Brooklyn Heights, 44131; one weekend in October; 661-7818)

This festival includes arts and crafts, farm animals, prizes, and special events for children.

(See also: Specialty Growers, chapter 3.)

Sunnybrook Farm Fall Herb Fair

(9448 Mayfield Rd., Chesterland, 44026; one weekend in September; 729-7232)

Come for talks and demonstrations, about twenty booths of gifts and crafts created by artists and specialists, contests, games, and food.

(See also: Gardens Open to the Public, chapter 1; Specialty Growers, chapter 3.)

Western Reserve Herb Society Fair

(The Garden Center of Greater Cleveland, 11030 East Blvd., Cleveland, 44106; one Saturday early in October; 721-1600)

This popular fundraising fair offers a wide variety of herbal products, decorations, and foods as well as herb-related demonstrations.

(See also: Gardens Open to the Public, chapter 1; General Horticultural Organizations, chapter 4.)

World's Largest Gourd Show

(one weekend in early autumn at the Morrow County Fairgrounds, Mount Gilead; 419-946-3302)

If you want to try something really different, go to this huge show to see mountains of gourds—made into lights, dolls, bowls, wind chimes, hats—plus other food and festivities.

HOME AND GARDEN TOURS

Northeast Ohio has many lovely residential gardens, each with a story to tell about landscaping, soil preparation, plant growth, and troubleshooting. One of the best ways to find out the whys and hows behind a garden is to take garden tours organized by communities, plant societies, or garden clubs. Some of these are listed here.

Chippewa Garden Club Home and Garden Tour
(7411 Old Quarry Ln., Brecksville, 44141)
This Brecksville-based club often sponsors a biannual weekend home and garden tour that helps finance community projects and scholarships.

Cleveland Rose Society
(contact Jim Wickert, 696-5729)
If you like roses, see if you can tag along when the society visits some of the members' gardens in full bloom.
(See also: Plant Societies, chapter 4.)

Cuyahoga County Cooperative Extension Services
(3200 W. 65th St., Cleveland; 44102; 631-1890)
You can tour the Extension's vegetable, herb, and perennial gardens from 10 a.m. to noon Thursdays and have your questions answered by Master Gardeners.

Dahlia Society of Ohio
(contact Monica Rini, 461-4190)
The Dahlia Society sometimes allows guests to join their annual summer garden tour and see glorious dahlias blooming at the homes of Dahlia Society members.
(See also: Plant Societies, chapter 4.)

The Garden Center of Greater Cleveland
(11030 East Blvd., Cleveland, 44106; 721-1600)
The Garden Center offers periodic tours of local gardens, gardens within a day's drive, and sometimes gardens in other countries.

Hudson Garden Club House and Garden Pilgrimage
(P.O. Box 651, Hudson, 44236)
This active and experienced club puts on one of the most popular home and garden tours.

Northern Ohio Perennial Society
(contact Eva Sands, 371-3363, or Betty McRainey, 732-9155)
This plant society often tours members' gardens during the summer.
(See also: Plant Societies, chapter 4.)

Medina County Fall Foliage Tour
(contact the Medina County Convention and Visitors Bureau, 124 W. Lafayette Rd., Medina, 44256; 722-5502)
This October outing features farms, gardens, and museums in rural Medina County.

~

Horticultural Professionals and Suppliers

Even if you are a dedicated do-it-yourselfer, you may eventually run out of time or expertise. Very few of us can do everything we would like with our own bare hands; we sometimes need help. For example, I do most of my own garden work, designing and tending my landscape and starting most of my vegetables and flowers from seed. I even build stone walls and rock gardens. But when it comes to heavy work like hauling soil and trees, intricate stuff such as building a stone patio, or exacting tasks like grafting evergreens, I call in professional help. Whether it's brains, brawn, or supplies you need, there are a wide array of horticultural professionals to choose from.

Evaluating the Project and the Professional

Once you recognize that you need help, you have to figure out who can handle the job. For nearly every task that needs doing around a yard, there are several kinds of professionals you can employ, from highly skilled specialists to day laborers.

The hard part is finding the right balance of skill, education, versatility, and cost.

For example, to build a stone patio or walk you can use a stonemason who specializes in stonework or a landscape contractor who does some construction in addition to planting, pruning, mowing, and other jobs. Your decision here may depend on the complexity of the project, the size of your budget, how long each company will take to do the job, and whether the contractor has the right experience.

If you are looking for someone to handle your lawn maintenance, you can use a landscape maintenance company, a lawn-care service, or neighborhood kid with a lawn mower. Each may approach the task from a slightly different perspective and complete the job in different ways. For instance, the neighborhood kid may be the least expensive but usually is also unskilled and won't know when to apply certain products, when to let the grass grow longer or when to cut it shorter, or when pests and diseases may be causing problems. A turf specialist from a lawn-care service will know all of these things but may not be able to help you with your flower garden or shrub pruning. A landscape maintenance company can tend to the other jobs around the yard but may not be as up-to-date on turf technology.

Once you decide the kind of service you need, check the qualifications of suppliers before giving them a deposit or setting them free in your yard. Learn what it is that a certain company does best, find out if they stand behind their work, and ask for several references. Look at some of the work they have done and be sure you like it. Also, will they stick to the price they quote you? Do you need to be at home to supervise, or is there a project supervisor who understands what you want and will see that it is done to your satisfaction? Has the company been in business long or might they disappear overnight? Is the company certified to sell you nursery stock or apply pesticides? Are their workers insured in case accidents happen? Does the company belong to a professional organization that keeps them informed of new developments? Ask these questions when the company salesman comes to call and before you sign a contract. And, finally, it is wise to get several estimates whenever you are contemplating major projects.

Local Professional Organizations

One sign that horticultural professionals are serious about what they do is membership in one or more of the dozens of national horticultural organizations. Three major groups that have active local chapters in the greater Cleveland area are:

Ohio Landscapers Association
(P.O. Box 170, Richfield, 44286; 659-9755)

Probably the most visible local association for horticultural professionals, the Ohio Landscapers Association includes landscapers, nurserymen, and designers, most of whom are from northeast Ohio (all the 1992 officers and board of directors are in the 216 area code). OLA members come from large and small companies, but all must be recommended by another member of the association and all must prove they hold the necessary licenses for spraying or for buying nursery stock wholesale and selling it retail. Representatives of some of the top local landscaping companies hold positions on committees or as officers.

The OLA provides plenty of opportunities for members and nonmembers to learn more about the field. The association sponsors a landscape design short course that gives new designers the fundamentals they need to begin designing landscapes. Other programs focus on new plants, new techniques, new products, and employee management methods. The OLA puts out a sophisticated monthly magazine, *The Growing Concern*, in which members share ideas, technology, and problems.

Design Network
(1506 Maple Rd., Cleveland Heights, 44121)

Many of the area's independent landscape designers belong to the Design Network, an idea-swapping organization that is loosely allied with the Association of Professional Landscape Designers. The group meets bimonthly in members' homes for programs and round-table discussions about plants, drawing techniques, construction, lighting, and garden products.

The Design Network is one place to find an independent designer, most of whom do not advertise. For a listing of designers' names and specialties, send a self-addressed, stamped envelop to the address above.

Western Reserve Section, Ohio Chapter
American Society of Landscape Architects
(1069 W. Main St., Westerville, 43081; 614-895-2222)

This organization brings together landscape architects from the greater Cleveland area for dinner meetings, instructional programs, and workshops at architecturally interesting locations around town. "Joining ASLA is not mandatory for a landscape architect, but a lot of landscape architects do belong because that is how you keep in touch with what's going on," said Bill Boron, former secretary of the Ohio Chapter of the ASLA. ASLA members can keep up with design trends, new materials, and creative alternatives used locally and nationally.

LANDSCAPE SPECIALISTS:
WHO DOES WHAT?

While most people would not consider making a long-term investment without the advice of a stockbroker or financial counselor, few are as organized when it comes to their own landscape. Like a closet, a yard can become a collection of random but costly odds and ends without function.

Imagine that instead of looking like an outdoor flea market, your yard could effectively increase your home's living space. You could entertain, swim, barbecue, play, and relax in comfort outdoors. Your landscape could also make your time indoors more enjoyable by giving you a pleasant view or more privacy. In addition, should you decide to sell your home, an attractive yard will help it sell more quickly and for a better price.

Obviously, making the most of your yard requires careful planning. It can involve as much strategy as investing in the stock market or preparing for retirement, and can require major amounts of time and money—good reasons to consider getting professional advice.

The cost need not be prohibitive. A landscape plan can be free, provided you pay for the installation. Or a plan can cost over $1,000. The cost depends upon the complexity of the job, which, in turn, will influence whether you should call upon a landscape architect, designer, or contractor.

Landscape Architects

Landscape architects must be registered with the state of Ohio and have a college degree in landscape architecture. Their academic training emphasizes architecture, urban planning, and civil engineering. Many landscape architecture firms concentrate on large residential, commercial, institutional, and government design. Some landscape architects, however, work on more modest projects as well. Some full-service landscape companies, those that design as well as build, have landscape architects on staff to work on hardscape such as roads, pools, bridges, and fencing. Design fees can range from $40 per hour, for an unregistered landscape architect, up to about $100 per hour.

Unless your yard needs a lot of grade changes or major construction, you may not need a landscape architect. If what you want is a good planting plan, a landscape architect may not fill the bill; most are not as well versed in plants as designers (though there are always exceptions).

Landscape Designers

Unlike landscape architects, landscape designers often come from horticultural backgrounds or have a two-year associate degree in landscape design. They tend to be knowledgeable about plants and have a good feel for aesthetics. Anyone can call himself a designer, however, so it is wise to check an individual's background before you sign a contract.

Designers' fees are easier on the budget than those of architects. They range from about $25 to $50 per hour. A simple plan may take only a few hours. On the other hand, a landscape carefully tailored to fit your lifestyle now as well as ten years in the future will require more frequent sessions with the designer. Irrigation systems, lighting, drainage, patios, decks, and other construction will also take time to design. Some designers also will consult for a fee without drawing an actual plan. They will walk around your yard with you and help you decide which plants should stay and which should go. You can do the actual planting yourself or hire a landscape contractor to undertake the designer's suggestions.

Landscape designers work either as part of a design/build team or independently. Independents may provide you with a plan with no further commitments or help. They also may put it out to bid. Many prefer to oversee construction, a form of quality control that is worth paying for. Some specialize in specific types of projects, such as herb or perennial gardens. Others will plan the entire yard.

Landscape Contractors

The third type of landscape service to consider is the landscape contractor, who can install from existing plans. In some states, a landscape contractor must have a degree in landscape architecture, but in Ohio that is not necessary or common.

Sometimes, a landscape contractor's crew may be certified as landscape technicians by the Ohio Nurserymen's Association. "Everyone in our landscape division takes the certification test," said Richard Kay, owner of Breezewood Gardens. "It brings a certain amount of professionalism with it. Before taking the test, a person gets a detailed book and six months to study. Those employees who have passed the test take more pride in what they do."

In the next few years you also may see landscape contractor managers and owners certified by the Association of Landscape Contractors of America, a national group in which a few of the more successful local contractors participate.

Legally, certification is not necessary to install or maintain gardens, nor is any background in design required. Anyone with a truck or a lawn mower can go into landscaping. Consequently, not all contractors are qualified to design. Some prefer to install an independent designer's work; others specialize in maintenance only.

"Having landscape contractors design a landscape can be a

real shot in the dark," says Lee Behnke, a landscape architect. "They may use things in their inventory they want to move out, or they can overdo on colored or variegated foliage and weeping habits."

"Everyone needs to know their own limits," agrees Steve Pattie of the Pattie Group, a full-service landscaper.

Landscape contractors traditionally have been the labor end of a landscape. Today, however, many larger contractors also have their own design departments. Design/build firms may design for an additional fee or for the price of installation. Others will design for "free." This is a sales tool, and, though it may sound like a bargain, many design professionals warn that you should not expect to keep the plan unless you sign up for installation. The design costs may be hidden in the labor fee or the markup on plants.

Affiliated Professionals

A variety of affiliated horticultural professionals exist to fill a range of gardening and landscape needs, including:

• *Compost and Soil Supply*
There are bulk suppliers of soil, compost, mulch, and sometimes stone and brick. From them, you can buy by the truckload. Look under topsoil or stone in the Yellow Pages for commercial sources. Or, you can buy leaf compost from the independent and nonprofit Greater Cleveland Ecology Program (687-1266), which collects landscape and garden waste from several communities and markets the resulting Cuyahoga Leaf Humus. Also, several cities and townships offer their own compost: the city of Solon (248-1155) gives finished humus away free to its residents; Westlake (871-3300) and Bay Village (871-2200) jointly sell and deliver finished compost within their city limits.

- *Garden Lighting*

You can have garden lighting installed by electricians, landscapers, or garden lighting specialists. Rick Tomko, owner of Site Illuminations in Newbury, is a landscape architect who specializes in site lighting. "My background lets me combine design capabilities with the technical and engineering experience of electrical contractors. Usually you get one or the other. The electricians might give you more functionality with little design; the landscaper might give you all design without current lamp technology. Since the lighting field changes on a daily basis, a company has to focus only on lighting to stay abreast of those advances."

Tomko recommends including lighting in the master plan for new homes and landscapes so the underground wiring can go in before the finished grading is done. Then you can put the lighting fixtures in after the plants are installed. Likewise, he suggests, run the wires indoors before the drywall is installed so the switches are properly placed.

- *Interior Plantscaping*

To install a few planters in a sunroom, develop an indoor atrium at an office, or maintain indoor plantings in a commercial atrium or a mall, you can get help from a specialist: an interior plantscaper.

"Interior work uses a different skill set for plant identification, maintenance, and care," says Nancy Silverman, owner of Plantscaping, Inc. "Even diseases are totally different from outdoors. It's a unique industry in its own."

A few universities offer horticulture programs specializing in interior plantscaping, and some community or technical schools, such as the Agricultural Technical Institute (see Adult Education in chapter 2), offer a two-year associate degree in interior plantscaping.

Beyond university training, many companies train their own maintenance staffs. "We have good luck training horticultural technicians who maintain plantings. Since Hurricane Andrew damaged most of the plant nurseries in Florida, we are really working on maintenance because some plants are just unavailable, especially the big stuff for the malls," Silverman said.

Mary Blaha from Interior Green Corporation said, "Most of our technicians are not horticulture graduates but are trained in-house by a manager who has a degree. I've trained a lot of people—enough to know it takes a special kind of person to work with plants. They have to recognize when a plant is failing and to know what to do."

Company-trained interior landscape technicians and, through a separate test, interior landscape professionals can be certified by the Interior Landscape Division of the Association of Landscape Contractors of America (the same certification previously available through the National Council for Interior Horticulture).

• Irrigation

Curtis Straubhaar, designer for Irrigation Supply, Inc. in Warrensville Heights, says irrigation specialists can consult with the landscape contractor who will be designing an irrigation system and install it with specialized machinery that leaves minimal disturbance in existing landscapes.

"Compared to landscape contractors, irrigation specialists are better versed in water conservation and application rates for different soils and plants. They can adapt the systems, using microsystems for small beds, or adjust the watering schedule according to the weather. We can tell contractors which irrigation nozzles to apply for the most efficient water application in the least amount of time with the least cost," Straubhaar said.

Some irrigation specialists are certified by the national Irrigation Association, which gives different tests to certify workers for residential, commercial, or golf-course irrigation.

• *Stone and Brick Work*
If you want to build an elaborate patio or walk that will require a specialist, you can look for stone- or brick-masons, who are part of the building trade and not commonly used for home landscapes. Because union bricklayers seldom take on smaller home landscaping projects, according to Solon-based stonemason Sal Fusco, only a few freelance stone- and brick-masons in this area are available to make patios and walkways.

The alternative to which most people turn today is landscape contractors who will work with brick, stone, or prefabricated interlocking paving blocks. These contractors may not have a background in stone and masonry work and may therefore lack some of the knowledge and skill of the specialists. "Furthermore," said Fusco, "most have to start from precut stone, which is less efficient than stone that is cut to fit the job."

• *Tree Care*
Arborists specialize in woody plants and may be the only kind of garden professional you can get to climb up in a tree or use a power saw, because of the high insurance costs of doing either. "Tree work is a specialty. Landscape crews who work on the ground are the artists; the guys in the trees are the daredevils—a breed of their own. Most of them would rather be up in the trees, even though they have to hold on with one hand and saw with the other—a dangerous job," said Fred Robinson, consulting arborist in Kirtland. You may want to use arborists to prune or remove a large tree, shape rare or disease-prone woody plants, help you select or plant trees and shrubs properly, control insects, or do other jobs that require

a solid background in woody plants.

Some of the larger landscape contractors or maintenance firms may have a crew of arborists as well as landscape crews; other companies specialize only in tree care. In either case, anyone can call themselves an arborist. To be sure skill lies behind the name, look for a crew that has at least one member certified by the International Society of Arboriculture.

Under certain circumstances, you also may need to use a consulting arborist. Consulting arborists are members of the American Society of Consulting Arborists, which admits new members only after they are approved by two existing members. ASCA arborists are qualified to provide advice; they study problems, make plans and diagnoses, hazard assessments and appraisals—seldom climbing into trees themselves. You can find consulting arborists at some large firms that handle tree care. Or you can hire independents and have the actual work done by the lowest or most qualified bidder.

To locate arborists in the Yellow Pages, look under Tree Care.

• *Turf Care*
If you like an emerald-green lawn of beautiful turf, then you know that keeping a lawn manicured takes considerable time and skill. For that reason, some horticulturists specialize in this field, taking care of golf courses, public parks, and baseball and football fields in addition to serving with lawn-care companies.

Dr. Bruce Augustin, the agronomist who handles education programs for Lesco, Inc., a lawn products supplier in Rocky River, says some turf specialists have horticulture or agronomy degrees. "There is a wide range of backgrounds in the lawn-care business, from trained agronomists to business people from other backgrounds," Augustin said. "In most big companies, there is a Ph.D. on staff, but some smaller companies also are run by Ph.D. horticulturists. The quality of the service they supply depends a lot on the individual."

Some people working in lawn care have two-year associate degrees or attend short courses to get some background. Any of them who apply pesticides must be tested and certified with the state of Ohio. Some companies belong to the Professional Lawn Care Association of America or the Ohio Turf Grass Association, which are not selective about their membership but provide members with up-to-date information on new practices.

In addition to lawn specialists, some landscape contractors (who mostly install plants) will mow lawns, too. And the middlemen—grounds maintenance crews—can apply lawn chemicals, mow, and maintain plantings.

PLANT SOURCES

In spring it seems as though everywhere you turn, people are selling plants. Pot after pot is lined outside of department stores, discount houses, and grocery stores, as well as the more traditional garden centers, nurseries, and greenhouses. Rather than buy the first plant that you see, find out what to expect from these vendors. Take possible limitations into account so you can be sure you get a healthy plant and good advice for keeping it healthy.

Grocery Stores, Discount Houses, Department Stores

These vendors do not specialize in plants, so don't expect them to answer your questions knowledgeably. You may, however, be able to find lower prices here because such chain stores buy in bulk. But the pressure is on you to know which plant will work well and whether it is healthy before you buy.

The plants may be of decent quality, if they were good plants to start with and have been tended well during shipping and stocking on shelves. But sometimes they have suffered a bit.

Always look closely at plants such as these before you buy. Be sure you know what cultivar you need; do your homework before you shop so you don't end up taking home something that will grow too big or flower in the wrong color. Then check to be sure the plant is labeled with the cultivar name; many are not and may be something less desirable. Be sure the leaf color is bright and appropriate for the type of plant, which shows that it has not suffered major setbacks in earlier life. Look under the leaves and along the stems to be sure insect pests are not clustered in hidden nooks.

Roots are harder to evaluate unless you remove the plant from the pot, a practice most stores frown upon. A plant will grow more vigorously if the roots are not overcrowded; ideally they will not be emerging through the pot holes and they certainly shouldn't be wound around and around inside the pot, a condition called root-bound. It's hard to get a plant to recover and grow when its roots are old and tangled.

Garden Centers

These full-service establishments are convenient because most carry supplies, fertilizers, tools, and may even offer landscape services. Better yet, they specialize in plants and related items so you know the management and buyers have thought about the kind of plants they carry and offer only cultivars that they feel are good for this area.

Many garden centers also offer sound advice on planting, pruning, or fertilizing to accompany your purchases. During the spring rush, however, or during off-hours the salespeople may not be trained horticulturists. If you need advice, look for the most reputable garden centers or call ahead and drop in at a time the manager or horticulturist is in and available.

Unlike nurseries and greenhouses (described in the next section), garden centers buy plant stock from wholesale growers, although a few growers also have garden centers at their production facility (see Specialty Growers in this chapter). When plants come from different growers, they may vary. For instance, I once was trying to find a couple of 'Blue Girl' holly bushes, the kind with blue-green leaves and red berries. At one garden center, I saw three very different looking shrubs all called 'Blue Girl'. I thought the labeling had to be wrong because one was quite short with few leaves but many berries, one was tall and lanky with leaves that were more green than blue, and another was shorter with darker leaves. Upon inquiring, I learned they all were 'Blue Girl' but from different growers. They were of different ages and had been fertilized in different ways; some were grown indoors and others had been kept outdoors; some were in containers and others were field dug and balled and burlapped. All of these factors changed their appearance and might affect their garden performance.

When you don't know who grew the plants offered at a garden center, try to find out if they come from local sources or are shipped in from the South or West Coast. Plants propagated from stock that grows naturally in warmer climates can be less hardy than the same species that grow in USDA zone 5 (see Climate in chapter 5) or cooler climates.

Despite the variations in origin of the plants, some garden centers will warranty their plants for a season or a year after purchase—if you keep the receipts. You can save yourself replacement costs on big purchases if you seek out these places.

Nurseries

Establishments that grow their own plants know how to make them grow well. And most growers are delighted to share what they know with you—as long as you don't ask during the busy spring season. Some will seek out the hardiest, or the showiest, or the newest cultivars for certain locations or certain purposes; they take pride in the plants they can present to you. Since anyone can legally grow and sell plants, however, you will have to choose nurserymen who know what they're doing. Some smaller or backyard nurseries may have limited plant selections and may not be able to advise you as well as an educated garden center salesperson. You also may have to travel elsewhere to buy tools or accessories.

Greenhouses

Indoor growing facilities are geared mostly to growing houseplants and holiday and annual flowers or to propagating hardy plants indoors. They are excellent places to find flowering plants or houseplants without working through middlemen. Some greenhouses, however, do not grow their own plants but merely keep them going after they are shipped from Florida or some other warm place. Also, some nurseries have greenhouses; some greenhouses have outdoor garden beds, too—so you occasionally can get the advantage of homegrown greenhouse items from vendors who do not necessarily call themselves greenhouses.

Mail Order

In addition to buying locally, you can order a great variety of plants—including many unusual ones—through the mail.

There is nothing wrong with this, as long as you buy from a reputable company, but the plants usually are smaller and have to endure shipping (and you have to endure the shipping and handling costs). For more information on mail-order nurseries, see the huge catalog file at The Garden Center library or the books *The Mail Order Gardener* (by Hal Morgan, 1988, Harper & Row, New York, NY) and *Gardening By Mail* (by Barbara J. Barton, 1990, Houghton-Mifflin, Boston, MA).

SPECIALTY GROWERS

A number of local plant growers are situated in northeast Ohio, though you may have to travel some distance to reach them because few remain in Cleveland. Some growers will save you the drive and let you order what you want from a catalog and then ship the plants by mail. But if you have the time, it's fun and informative to drop in and inspect, or be inspired by, the plants. Here is a list of my favorite local (or nearly local) nurseries where you can also find:

• Breeders, who produce their own cultivars
• Display gardens, with plants in garden settings so you can see what a small potted plant will mature to look like
• Specialists, who concentrate on certain kinds of plants

Also, some growers will give tours and some have plant lists available. Beyond the growers mentioned here, there are many general and wholesale growers. A few of these wholesalers may sell a small percentage of their plants retail, but they prefer not to deal with individual customers and are therefore not listed.

Art Form Nurseries

(15656 Rte. 306, Bainbridge, 44023; 338-8102; display gardens;
spring plant list available)

Art Form specializes in growing perennials outdoors in one-gallon containers that are larger than most mail-order plants. They carry a large but fluctuating stock, including many of the popular newer cultivars. You can get inspired as you drive in beside the long perennial border that extends down to an interesting rock garden at the sales yard.

Barco Sons, Inc./Liberty Gardens

(935 State Rte. 18, Medina, 44256; 722-3038)

Liberty Gardens, a garden center, is the retail outlet for bedding plants produced by the wholesale growers Barco Sons, Inc., a family who have been in the greenhouse business for three generations.

Betzel Greenhouse

(3225 North Ridge Rd., Lorain, 44055; 277-4470)

This wholesale greenhouse grower dabbles in retail sales, devoting half of one greenhouse range to tempt us gardeners. They grow seasonal flowers, such as poinsettias and Easter plants, foliage plants for the house, and annual flowers for springtime. A second greenhouse range located in Avon is strictly wholesale.

Bluestone Perennials

(7211 Middle Ridge Rd., Madison, 44057; 800-852-524 or 428-1327;
free mail-order catalog)

This nursery specializes in selling young perennial plants produced in a high-tech greenhouse, and at low prices. They sell by catalog but have reasonable shipping fees, and the plants are guaranteed to arrive in good shape and grow, or they will be replaced. Such plants may not bloom on time the first year—and will be slower to claim their rightful position in the garden—but they catch up with larger plants fast.

Borlin Orchids
(9885 Johnnycake Ridge Rd., Concord-Mentor, 44060; 354-8966 or 800-284-9518; delivery available in Cuyahoga County)

Borlin's is the only greenhouse in this area that specializes primarily in orchids, both potted plants and cut flowers. Although the owner, Lou Borlin, does not start his own orchids, he often keeps plants for years and has a lifetime of experience to share. Borlin has a display area that features all the orchids that are in bloom at any particular time and a separate garden center and florist shop.

Burton Floral & Garden, Inc.
(13020 Kinsman Rd., Burton; 834-4135)

This greenhouse is a bit of a haul for some, but it's worthwhile if you are looking for new and different cultivars such as ivy geraniums, trailing dusty-miller, felicia daisies, as well as perennials, poinsettias, chrysanthemums, and Easter flowers.

Carter's Greenhouse
(11152 Crackle Rd., Mantua, 44255; 543-4340)

This new facility replaces Carter Zane's old Blossom Basket greenhouse that was on Route 44 in Geauga County. Zane expects to be open again as of 1993; call to see what the status of the greenhouse is before driving out there. He will be continuing his tradition of growing unusual cut flowers and specialty bedding plants, but with an expanded selection of plants grown in outdoor beds. Zane can give you good tips for using the plants he grows and may surprise you with some unusual selections.

Chagrin Valley Nurseries

(1370 River Rd., Gates Mills, 44040; 423-3363; tours available for garden groups with advance reservation—contact Victor Mastrangelo; plant list available in spring)

This is a favorite east-side nursery; it is inclined toward chemical-free growing and carries 400 different kinds of plants—about 50 percent homegrown. You can tag the plant you want in the field and have the nurserymen custom-dig it for you while you enjoy a view of the wooded Chagrin River Valley from the nursery.

Champion Garden Towne

(3717 N. Ridge Rd., P.O. Box 21, Perry, 44081; 259-2811)

Champion Garden Towne is the retail outlet for Lake County Nursery, Inc., one of the area's largest wholesale nurseries. You can find or order anything from the catalog at Champion Garden Towne, including new plants like the Meidiland roses and Lake County Nursery's own cultivars of crab apple 'Harvest Gold' and seedless *Acer* 'Celebration' (a hybrid between red and silver maple). Champion Garden Towne also sells annuals, perennials, ornamental grasses, fresh produce, cut flowers, gifts, gourmet foods, and statues.

Just down the road, you can enjoy Lake County Nursery's plants in the Mary Elizabeth Garden (see Gardens Open to the Public, chapter 1).

Corso's Flower and Garden Center

(3404 Milan Rd., Sandusky, 44870; 419-626-0789)

If you're visiting Cedar Point, drop in to find some unusual perennials at this good grower's facility. Corso's propagates over three hundred varieties of perennial plants, mostly sold in four-and-a-half inch or one-gallon pots (a few are bigger). Some of the best finds here are hard-to-get hardy ferns;

hostas; tetraploid daylilies; bearded, Japanese, and Siberian iris; and monkshood. Check out the perennial border that edges the parking area for new ideas to use at home. Corso's also propagates bedding annuals and grows aquatic plants.

Daisy Hill Greenhouses, Inc.
(34050 Hackney Rd., Moreland Hills, 44022; 247-4422)

This was the estate greenhouse in the old Daisy Hill estate of the Van Sweringen brothers, who developed much of Shaker Heights. The greenhouse was converted to a commercial greenhouse about fifty years ago while houses sprang up around it. Now you will find the greenhouse hidden in a lovely and exclusive residential area. The staff continues to do an excellent job of growing herbs and perennials, topiary, indoor flowering and foliage plants, and annual flowers in hanging baskets.

Dean's Greenhouse and Flower Shop
(3984 Porter Rd., Westlake; 871-2050)

This greenhouse is devoted primarily to growing geraniums and it is complemented by a garden center and florist shop, and a small herb garden that you can wander through.

Falconskeape Gardens
(7359 Branch Rd., Medina, 44259; 723-4966; plant list available)

Ameri-Hort Research, the nursery division of Falconskeape Gardens, offers lilacs hybridized by the late Father John Fiala, founder of Falconskeape. They are not touted as mildew resistant but do resist other lilac diseases, and they feature exceptionally showy flower clusters. A couple particularly caught my eye. 'Albert F. Holden', named after the founder of Holden Arboretum, has deep violet blooms with a silvery blush on the reverse of the petals. 'Little Boy Blue' is a miniature that reaches only four to five feet tall and carries sky-blue flowers.

(See also: Gardens Open to the Public, chapter 1; General Horticultural Organizations, chapter 4.)

The Garden Center of Greater Cleveland
(11030 East Blvd., Cleveland, 44106; 721-1600)

The Garden Center has local growers custom-grow a wide assortment of the best cultivars of flowers—annual and perennial—for their annual May plant sale. They also stock other garden items for this fun-filled sale.

(See also Gardens Open to the Public, chapter 1; Adult Education, Children's Gardening Programs, Horticultural Therapy, Garden Libraries, and Special Events in chapter 2; General Horticultural Organizations, chapter 4.)

Garden Place
(6776 Heisley Rd., Mentor, 44060; 255-3705; catalog available for a small fee)

This mail-order retailer (which also grows wholesale for many national mail-order nurseries) offers over a thousand varieties of perennials, including many of the newest and best types. They are shipped bare root in spring, which makes them a bit trickier to plant than those grown in containers. For more information on planting bare-root material, see *Foolproof Planting* (by Anne Moyer Halpin, 1990, Rodale Press, Emmaus, PA).

Girard Nurseries
(Box 428, 6839 North Ridge [East Rte. 20], Geneva; 44041; 466-2881; free catalog available; display gardens)

The Girard family propagates and grows many types of trees and shrubs; they also breed evergreen and deciduous azaleas, rhododendrons, dwarf conifers, and evergreens, such as the patented juniper 'Saybrook Gold'. They also offer bonsai starts, small grafts of rare species like weeping Nootka cypress, silver noble fir, Gentsch white hemlock, and Japanese dragon-eye pine. You can order small items by mail or go there and pick up larger plants.

If you make the trip, visit the display gardens. You can walk grass paths between mixed island beds of perennials, shrubs, and trees (especially lovely and large specimens of rare nursery stock), and stop at a gazebo and sunken arbor. You are welcome to visit their 64 growing houses that are open to the public.

Gilson Gardens, Inc.
(3059 U.S. Rte. 20, P.O. Box 277, Perry 44081; 259-4845; free catalog available)

This nursery, with a large attached garden center and florist shop, specializes in ground covers—over a hundred different types, including European ginger, Bethleham sage (*Pulmonaria* species), hardy cactus (*Opuntia*), lamium, epimedium—and low-growing perennials such as 'Palace Purple' coralbells, coreopsis 'Moonbeam', and hosta. You can buy their home-grown plants at their garden center or order small plants from a mail-order catalog.

Granger Gardens
(1060 Wilbur Rd., Medina, 44256; 239-2349; plant list available if you send a self-addressed, stamped envelope)

This greenhouse has been hybridizing standard and pinwheel African violets for decades and now sells their cultivars internationally. You will be surprised by the diversity available in African violets today, which you can see as you wander through the Granger greenhouse range. Owner Jim Eyerdom says the most popular varieties include powder-blue flowered 'Wonderland', which has been voted most popular several years running by the African Violet Society of America, and the Fantasy series, violets with different-colored speckles on their flowers.

Hansen's Greenhouse
(8781 Columbia Rd., Olmsted Falls, 44138; 235-1961)
Look in this three-quarter acre greenhouse range for floral crops such as poinsettias, flowers for Easter and Mother's Day, and for flats of annual flowers.

Hirt's Greenhouse and Flowers
(13867 Pearl Rd., Strongsville, 44136; 238-8200)
Hirt's is propagating many of its own plants to provide hard-to-find cultivars of vegetables, herbs, and perennials. You will find over 50 different kinds of herbs, including 15 cultivars of basil alone, 75 varieties of seed-grown tomatoes (many of which are heirlooms), and over 100 types of perennials. Beyond what is grown in-house, Hirt's offers a range of garden center goods.

Holden Arboretum
(9500 Sperry Rd., Kirtland, 44060; 946-4400; call for sale dates)
Holden Arboretum offers some homegrown wildflowers during their spring fund-raising sale, usually held in early May. In past years these native plants have been propagated from Ohio wildflowers; more recently, the arboretum has been buying some plants from out-of-state propagators, which natural-areas coordinator Brian Parsons says can be even better quality than Holden's own plants. You will also find cultivars of wildflowers such as *Tiarella* 'Oak Leaf', a distinctive form of foamflower, and 'Fuller's White' woodland

phlox. The Holden staff, however, will continue to stock some local plants, especially seedlings or divisions taken from the wildflower garden. They also have trees, shrubs, and perennials on hand. (See also: Gardens Open to the Public, chapter 1; Adult Education, Children's Gardening Programs, Horticultural Therapy, Garden Libraries, and Special Events in chapter 2; General Horticultural Organizations, chapter 4.)

Kaiser's Greenhouse and Flower Shop
(2157 Northview Rd., Rocky River, 44116; 333-5650)

A one-acre greenhouse area of poinsettias, annuals and geraniums, plus a garden center and florist area.

Lake Erie Nature and Science Center
(28728 Wolf Rd., Bay Village, 44140; 871-2900)

This privately operated nature center, located in the Metroparks' Huntington Reservation, has a spring plant sale, the Spring Thing, which offers annual and perennial plants and wildflowers, some of which are local. Call in early spring for the sale date.

Leeland Greenhouse
(24377 Royalton Rd., P.O. Box 1057, Columbia Station, 44028; 236-5891)

This four-and-a-half acre greenhouse range sells annual flowers, poinsettias, and Easter flowers wholesale and retail.

Lowe's Greenhouses and Gift Shop
(16540 Chillicothe Rd., Chagrin Falls, 44023; 543-5123; plant list available)

Lowe's grows unusual perennials, such as purple-leaved black snakeroot (*Cimicifuga racemosa* 'Atropurpurea') and toad lilies, and unusual annuals like poor-man's orchid (*Schizan-thus*) and several types of strawflowers. You are welcome to walk through the one-acre greenhouse, where you will see these and other flowers, including cut flowers such as lisianthus and blue Queen Anne's lace that are used in Lowe's florist shop. They also have a garden center area.

Maria Gardens Greenhouse
(20465 Royalton Rd., Strongsville, 44136; 238-7637 and 10301 W. 130th St., North Royalton, 44133; 582-4750)

Maria Gardens uses their own garden centers as retail outlets for the on-site greenhouses. The Strongsville location has a two-acre greenhouse; the North Royalton range has one-half acre under glass. They specialize in popular and traditional types of seasonal flowers, annuals, perennials, and foliage plants.

Meurer's Greenhouse
(4646 W. 11th St., Cleveland, 44109; 351-9338)

Talk about convenience, right in the heart of the city you'll find an acre of greenhouse filled with holiday plants and bedding annuals. They sell about half of their crops retail and the other half wholesale.

Moldovan's Gardens
(38830 Detroit Rd., Avon, 44011; 216-934-4993; catalog available)

Steve Moldovan, a former high-school horticulture teacher, his mother, Mary Moldovan, and Roy Woodhall sell their own hybrid daylilies and hosta, plus miniature daylilies from other breeders, through a mail-order catalog. Among their many hosta listings is Moldovan's 'Leprechaun' with yellow-chartreuse leaves that are only two by three inches long, and 'Monitor', with almost black-green leaves that grow nearly three feet high and six feet wide. Among daylilies,

Moldovan lists new lines of tetraploid (having twice the normal number of chromosomes, which can make flowers bigger and bolder) daylilies with purple, lavender, and pink flowers. The new hybrids cost between $100 and $150; earlier introductions can be less expensive. (See also: Gardens Open to the Public, chapter 1.)

Musial's Greenhouse

(5913 Avon-Belden Rd., North Ridgeville, 44039; 327-8855)

This greenhouse entices retail and wholesale customers in spring with hundreds of impressive hanging baskets of unusual plants. They also carry over twenty-five different kinds of geraniums, plus other bedding annuals, herbs, and perennials.

Perennials Preferred

(8360 Rte. 6, Kirtland; 256-2720; call for open hours and days)

This small retail nursery specializes in unusual perennials, miniatures, and alpines, including rare species of phlox, veronica and gentians, as well as trough gardens (small rocklike tubs used to grow tiny ornamental plants). A small display garden winds around a nearby pond, showing off the interesting textures and flower forms of the tiny creepers, plus a few bigger perennials. There is a variegated *Phlox* x *procumbens*, a sought-after 'Ballerina' hardy geranium, a dwarf *Inula*, and many others. Even though the garden is small, you can see a lot if you look closely.

Piazza Floral Greenhouse

(35638 Detroit Rd., Avon, 44011; 937-6888)

Piazza's two-acre greenhouse specializes in growing geraniums but also carries a variety of annual flowers in flats as well as holiday floral crops. They bring in foliage plants from Florida to grow to a larger size.

Quailcrest Farm

(2810 Armstrong Rd., Wooster, 44691; 345-6722; plant list available; workshops and programs avail. for garden-oriented groups)

This nursery/garden center (they don't grow everything themselves) is well known for its gift shops and display gardens, but also offers homegrown herbs, unusual indoor plants, and perennials. One growing field is devoted to perennials that you may select yourself and have the staff dig—an old-fashioned practice that is almost unheard of today. Other plants come in contemporary containers.

(See also: Gardens Open to the Public, chapter 1; Special Events, chapter 2.)

Quality Nursery

(U.S. Rte. 6 and Clay St., Montville, 44064; 968-3990; plant list available)

This nursery, an eclectic one-man-operation, though out of the way for many, is worth visiting if you're looking for unusual plants. During daylily season in July, owner Hal Boesger, Jr., holds a festival featuring hybrid daylilies of his own breeding and about three thousand other varieties. One especially notable cultivar is Boesger's 'Around in Black', a lemon-colored dark-throated rebloomer developed from 'Stella d'Oro'. Boesger also collects a large assortment of variegated plants and unusual species, such as eight-foot-tall late-flowering daylilies and bush clover (*Lespedeza thunbergii* 'Gibralter'), a perennial herb that displays a shrubby wall of flowers in mid-October.

Richardson's Farm Market and Greenhouse

(Brookpark and Schaaf roads, Cleveland, 44131; 661-7888)

A garden center and farm market back up to greenhouses that hold unusual indoor plants such as night-blooming cereus cactus, Cape primrose (*Streptocarpus* species), variegated hibiscus, and angel-wing begonias, succulents such as weeping notonia, and bedding annuals, including geraniums and impatiens. Chickens and cats roam the range, making a visit fun for kids.

Rosby Brothers Greenview Greenhouse
(42 East Schaaf Rd., Cleveland, 44131; 351-0850; tours available)
This old Schaaf Road greenhouse grows annuals, perennials, and poinsettias as well as pick-your-own strawberries and red raspberries. There is a garden center and compost facility that you can tour with advance reservations.

Shaker Lakes Regional Nature Center
(2600 South Park Blvd., Shaker Hts., 44120; 321-5935)
This nature center holds a spring plant sale, sponsored by the Friends of the Shaker Lakes Nature Center, that features annual flowers, vegetable plants, and homegrown perennial flower divisions, most of which can be ordered in advance of the sale. Contact the Center for an advance order form in early spring.

Silver Creek Farm
(7097 Allyn Rd., P.O. Box 254, Hiram, 44234; 562-4381, or 569-3487; group tours, talks, slide shows available with advance reservations)
This is an organic market garden where you can buy produce that has never been touched by garden chemicals.
(See also: Gardens Open to the Public, chapter 1;

Sunnybrook Farms and Homestead Division
(9448 Mayfield Rd., Chesterland, 44026; 729-7232; catalog avail.)
This is a large garden center area with a greenhouse range

devoted to growing about two hundred types of herbs, including many kinds of scented geraniums and mints, plus dozens of different ivies and hundreds of hosta. It's fun to combine browsing in the greenhouses and garden center with a stroll in the hosta garden.

(See also: Gardens Open to the Public, chapter 1; Adult Education, chapter 2.)

Sweet Bay Gardens
(9801 Stafford Rd., Auburn, 44023; 543-9396)

This small nursery is one of the few commercial enterprises to grow native plants for woodlands, wetlands, bog, and meadow gardens. They also have a fair number of exotic species that will do well in these habitats, too. Visits to the nursery are by appointment only.

Thibo Greenhouses
(7691 Avon-Belden Rd., North Ridgeville, 44039; 327-8151)

This 3.5-acre greenhouse sells primarily wholesale but will accept retail customers. It specializes in bedding plants, including 10 kinds of geraniums, and in hanging baskets.

William Tricker, Inc.—Water Garden
(7125 Tanglewood Dr., Independence; 524-3491)

If you want to see something different, visit this greenhouse of water plants and animals, a well-kept secret in Cleveland. Although Tricker's was founded in 1895, the company keeps a low profile because they don't advertise locally. Instead, they sell most of their stock by mail. But it's lots of fun to browse through the beds of water lilies that feature some of Tricker's own hybrids, such as pink-flowered 'Independence', rose-flowered 'Cleveland', and deep purple-flowered 'Blue Bird'.

Vanderbrook, Don
(Newbury; 371-0164)

Don Vanderbrook holds a spring plant sale of unusual flowers, many of which he grows in his own garden. The sale happens during one weekend in May. Call the office number listed here to find out the date and directions to his garden-plant sale.

(See also: Claystone Farm entry in Gardens Open by Appointment, chapter 1.)

Wade and Gatton Nurseries
(1288 Gatton Rock Rd., Bellville, 44813; 419-883-3191; perennials sold retail—other nursery stock is wholesale only; display garden)

This nursery is the farthest from Cleveland in this listing, but if you like hosta and other unusual perennials it is worth the drive. You can take I-71 south to Route 13 and follow charming country roads over rolling hills to this nursery, said to have the world's largest collection of hosta. Thousands of hosta plants are spread across several acres of gardens, nestled beneath a high canopy of oaks and pines. Grass paths and a trickling stream wind between the beds, which often are devoted to hosta cultivars developed by a single breeder. The soil in the beds is astonishing—rich in peat and perlite, which may account for the lush way the hosta grow.

In a sunnier area on a nearby hill, you also can see extensive collections of daylilies and an impressive bed of ornamental grasses. These and the hosta are interplanted with other perennial flowers, including such rare plants as Scotch thistle, variegated rhubarb, variegated phlox, and iris.

The perennials you can buy are divided out of these gardens or grown in one gallon or larger containers. Write to ask the nursery about the availability of cultivars you are looking for, and they will write back with the price and how they can ship it. Tell them if you are a member of a garden club or plant society to receive a small discount.

Wildwood Gardens
(14488 Rock Creek Rd., Chardon, 44024; 286-3714;
plant list available; will ship UPS)

In the midst of rural Geauga County lies one of the area's few bonsai nurseries and display gardens. They also grow alpine and rare plants. The nursery was begun over thirty years ago to finance the plant collection of Anthony Mihalic and now is operated by his son, Frank, who travels to the Orient to import bonsai every year. Mihalic also propagates and trains his own bonsai plants and teaches others to do the same. Some of the most interesting older bonsai plants and some intriguing alpines are displayed around a large tufa-rock garden behind the bonsai studio. For more information on how to take care of bonsai plants, look for Frank Mihalic's book, *The Art of Bonsai*, which is sold through the nursery.

Willotts, Dorothy and Tony
(26231 Shaker Blvd., Beachwood, 44122; 831-8662; catalog sales
only; can give slide lectures on irises)

These veteran breeders of irises specialize in dwarf types that bloom earlier than most bearded irises. They sell only by mail. Their list includes over a hundred of their own introductions. Some familiar sounding dwarfs include raspberry, amber and orange-flowered 'Falconskeape', light to full violet-blue flowered 'Geauga Lake', and yellow and brown striped 'Landerwood'. In the taller types, you can find cream, gold, and orange-yellow flowered 'Cedar Point' and ruffled cream, gold and brown flowered 'Pepper Pike'. The irises are shipped bare root in late summer.

(See also: Rockefeller Park Greenhouse entry in Gardens Open to the Public, chapter 1.)

Wood and Company, Inc.
(2267 Lee Rd., Cleveland Hts., 44118; 321-7557)
This garden center may be the only one in the area that imports its own flowering bulbs. Peter Brumbaugh, owner, deals with some of the smaller bulb growers in Holland, Israel, and other bulb-growing areas and buys only their best. He can tell you nearly anything you want to know about bulbs and will special order.

To find more local retail growers or generalists, look in area Yellow Pages under Nurseries or Greenhouses.

OTHER HORTICULTURAL SUPPLIERS

Other Specialists to Seek Out
In addition to fields directly linked to horticulture or landscaping, you can find goods for gardens at places you might not expect. For:

- Outdoor sculpture, Japanese lanterns, or weather vanes: look at art galleries and studios or museum shops
  - Terra-cotta pots and planters: consult pottery shops
  - Benches or tables: look at furniture and patio stores
  - Fountains: try plumbing dealers
  - Gazebos and garden houses: check at lumber stores
  - Gates or plant stands: look for wrought-iron blacksmiths

Mail-Order Supply
If you can't find what you want locally, check the many speciality catalogs. For a better idea of what catalogs are available, see the book *Gardening By Mail* (by Barbara J. Barton, 1990,

Houghton-Mifflin, Boston, MA) or check the catalog files in the library at The Garden Center of Greater Cleveland.

Some of the Better Vegetable and Flower Seed Catalogs

- W. Atlee Burpee and Co.
  (Warminster, PA 18974)
- The Cook's Garden
  (P.O. Box 535, Londonderry, VT 05148; small fee for catalog.)
  - Johnny's Selected Seeds
    (Foss Hill Road, Albion, ME 04910-9731)
  - Park Seed Company
    (Cokesbury Road, Greenwood, SC 29647-0001)
  - Pinetree Garden Seeds
    (Box 300, New Gloucester, ME 04260)
  - Shepherd's Garden Seeds
    (6116 Highway 9, Felton, CA 95081)
  - Thompson and Morgan
    (P.O. Box 1308, Jackson, NJ 08527)

CHAPTER FOUR

Horticultural Organizations

THERE ARE HUNDREDS OF local garden clubs, plant societies, and horticultural institutions that welcome new members. Gardeners join them for a variety of reasons: to make new friends who share common interests, to learn from veteran members or outside speakers, or to swap experiences—a therapeutic way to learn and grow.

There is great diversity in club organization and purpose. Some, like the Western Reserve Herb Society, are working clubs dedicated to learning, maintaining a display garden, and fund-raising throughout the year. Others mix service projects with planting talk, crafts, and events such as home tours and flower-arranging or fashion shows. Some are devoted to studying a certain kind or group of plants in depth; others touch on a wide range of related topics. Some include members from all across greater Cleveland; others are concentrated in a certain region. Some include a variety of different kinds of people; others cater to men or women, or younger or older members.

To give an idea of what kinds of organizations are out there, here is a lengthy list of those known to welcome new members. Not included are groups that get new members by invitation only or clubs that grow only by bringing in friends and aquaintances of existing members.

In nearly every case, visitors are welcome to attend club meetings and shows to meet the group and see how they operate before joining. You may not be able to attend special events or parties, however, until joining. Fees for plant society memberships tend to be very reasonable; they pay for the club operations and often a newsletter. As might be expected, horticultural institutions charge considerably more because they have to pay for their facilities and staff.

General Horticultural Organizations

Cleveland Waterfront Coalition
(401 Euclid Ave., The Arcade, Room 462, Cleveland, 44114; membership: $10 student/senior, $20 individual, $50 organization, $100 corporation; newsletter; 771-2666)

Although not strictly a horticultural organization, the Waterfront Coalition has attracted members from among local gardeners. They are working to give the public access to the ten miles of Lake Erie shoreline. There are about fifteen hundred members involved in fund-raising and activist aspects of this group.

Cleveland Zoological Society
(P.O. Box 609281, Cleveland, 44109; annual membership fee: $25 individual, $40 family, $30 senior couple, $17 senior single, $50 contributing, $100 sustaining, $500 patron, $100 gorilla giver; quarterly Zoo News; *contact Carol Olson, 661-6500)*

Membership in the Cleveland Zoological Society, a fund-raising and support group for the public zoo, brings discounted rates for rain forest admittance and free zoo admittance, invitations to special zoo parties, discounts at zoo shops and programs, and free admission to 90 other zoos nationwide. The quarterly *Zoo News* includes insights into how the zoo works, what's new, and educational articles on the zoo exhibits—stressing animals of course. (See also: Gardens Open to the Public, chapter 1.)

Clean-Land, Ohio

(1836 Euclid Ave., Suite 702, Cleveland, 44114; annual memberships available; quarterly newsletter; 696-2122)

Clean-Land, Ohio operates several urban gardening and environmental programs for Cleveland. City Side Gardens develops vacant lots into garden sites with perennial beds, trees, shrubs, ornamental grasses, bulbs, and lawn. Clean-Land Commons creates mini-parks, the largest of which is at Playhouse Square, between Huron and Euclid avenues. Between these two programs, over fifty city sites have now been rejuventated.

NeighborWoods promotes urban reforesting. Another program, called CleanScape, is dedicated to picking up litter downtown and in the Midtown Corridor; they removed 50,000 tons between 1981 and 1992. Classroom programs teach kids about recycling and litter prevention; Precycle! Cleveland tells adults about the importance of reducing waste by reusing and recycling items usually thrown away.

Community Gardening

People without space for a garden at their home, office, or apartment can lease a plot at a community garden. These occupy otherwise vacant land throughout much of greater Cleveland and give garden access—and a chance to socialize with other gardeners—to anyone who is interested.

Most of the community gardens are vacant-lot-sized and contain two to four gardens. Some of the larger ones are in Cleveland Heights, in Cleveland at 104th and Sandusky, and in Old Brooklyn at Ben Franklin Elementary School. The size and cost of community garden plots vary, said Dennis Rinehart, director of Seed to Shelf (a program that advises these gardeners), but the average cost is between $5 and $25.

Although community gardeners may form their own garden clubs, there is no community gardeners' society. Instead, they are supported by government organizations such as Seed to Shelf and the Summer Sprout Program (both included in this listing).

Friends of the Greenhouse, Inc.

(Rockefeller Park Greenhouse, 750 E. 88th St., Cleveland, 44108; 664-3103; meets the 2nd Wednesday of each month, 10 a.m. at the Greenhouse; annual membership fee: $20 student/senior, $25 individual, $30 couple, $40 family)

This fund-raising group organizes horticultural classes and garden parties that members can attend at discounted rates. The biggest project the Friends are tackling is raising enough money to expand the greenhouse lobby and provide space for sit-down dinners.

(See also: Gardens Open to the Public, chapter 1.)

Friends of Falconskeape Gardens

(7359 Branch Rd., Medina, 44259; 723-4966; plant list available; annual membership fee: $25 individual/family, $50 commercial/institutional, $400 lifetime; 723-4966)

For the price of membership, you can visit the grounds and attend concerts and special events. You receive a commemorative lilac and 10 percent discount on other plant or supply purchases.

(See also: Gardens Open to the Public, chapter 1; Specialty Growers, chapter 3.)

The Garden Center of Greater Cleveland

(11030 East Blvd., Cleveland, 44106; 721-1600; annual membership fee: $30 individual, $40 family, other levels available; monthly Garden Center Bulletin; 721-1600)

You can view the gardens, attend the shows, and look at the library books without joining The Garden Center, but by joining you help finance all the good things that go on there. You also can borrow library books, get discounts at the Trellis Shop, receive the information-packed *Bulletin*, and invitations to members-only events. Members get a 25 percent discount on classes and can consult with Garden Center horticulturists free of charge.

(See also: Gardens Open to the Public, chapter 1; Adult Education, Children's Gardening Programs, Horticultural Therapy, Garden Libraries, and Special Events, chapter 2; Specialty Growers, chapter 3.)

Gardenview Horticultural Park

(16711 Pearl Road, Rte. 42, Strongsville, 44136; 238-6653; annual membership fee: $25 to $49 for single or family, other levels available; 238-6653)

This nonprofit organization supports the extensive gardens and the horticultural library at Gardenview. Members may visit at any time free of charge and may use the library with advance reservations. Sustaining members may bring 10 free guest visitors.

(See also: Gardens Open to the Public, chapter 1.)

Hiram Community Gardens

(Box 402, Hiram, 44234-0402; annual membership fee: $15; spring newsletter; no phone)

This organization started in 1978 as a way to raise funds to maintain the network of public gardens in Hiram. The members are mostly residents of Hiram but others are welcome to donate and join. The funds allow the organization to hire college students who are trained by Jim and Jamie Barrow. "It's become a community effort rather than public or private," Barrow explained. "It's especially unique in such a tiny village, but people could easily see the improved quality of the environment and recognize its value."

(See also: Gardens Open to the Public, chapter 1.)

Holden Arboretum

(9500 Sperry Rd., Kirtland, 44060; 946-4400; annual membership fee: $40 family, $25 seniors, $75 contributing, $100 rare-plant testing program; $150 sustaining, and up; Arboretum Leaves *quarterly newsletter; 946-4400)*

Membership in this nonprofit arboretum includes use of the grounds free (including fishing and cross-country skiing), discounted rates for programs, and members-only parties. It also includes *Arboretum Leaves*—which always brings news of developments in the gardens and woodlands around Kirtland—a 10 percent discount at the gift shop, and a free guest pass.

(See also: Gardens Open to the Public, chapter 1; Adult Education, Children's Gardening Programs, Horticultural Therapy, Garden Libraries, and Special Events, chapter 2; Specialty Growers, chapter 3.)

Seed to Shelf Program of Cuyahoga County Cooperative Extension Service

(contact Dennis Rinehart, Extension Agent, Urban Gardening, 631-1890)

In 1978, this program was started to help community gardeners by providing information and organization for the slightly over two hundred community gardens in Cuyahoga

County. Extension Service agents and Master Gardeners train garden leaders, teaching them how to plant, control insects, and resolve conflicts. They supply low-cost soil testing kits, fact sheets, and food preservation classes. They also have rototillers that community gardeners can borrow. And they publish the *Seed to Shelf Newsletter*.

For other counties, contact the County Cooperative Extension Service (Geauga: 834-4656, Lake: 357-2582, Lorain: 322-0127, Medina: 725-4911, Summit: 497-1611).

Summer Sprout Program
Cleveland Department of Redevelopment
(contact Linda Park, real estate manager, 664-4089)

This city-sponsored institution, funded by Community Development Block Grants, supplies soil amendments, seeds, bedding plants, and soil tilling for people who want to garden on vacant land in the city of Cleveland. They also can arrange reduced price permits for gardeners who want to irrigate from nearby fire hydrants. All sites have a volunteer garden coordinator who serves as contact between the city and the garden.

Plant Societies

Camera Guild of Cleveland
(usually meets weekly, 8 p.m. Thursdays at The Garden Center of Greater Cleveland, except in summer when meetings are twice a month; annual membership fees: $25; monthly newsletter; contact Robert Schroeder, 449-1331)

Many gardeners like to capture what they have grown in photographs. Since good photography takes very different skills from growing roses or herbs, you may find you need to turn to more experienced photographers, like members of the Camera Guild, for help. There are approximately thirty members of this fifty-year-old group who meet regularly to critique photos and slides of nature and travel. They hold monthly competitions and sometimes sponsor group photography exhibits at places like The Garden Center.

Chagrin Valley Herb Society

(meets at 1 p.m. on the 3rd Thursday of most months at Bainbridge Library, Geauga County; annual membership fee: $10; contact Kathy Catani, 338-3986)

This group was organized to develop a public herb garden in eastern Geauga County. Presently, there are about forty members who tend the garden and have monthly programs and workshops—including one workshop for the public. They also hold an annual herbal luncheon and a plant sale on the Saturday before Mother's Day.

(See also: Gardens Open to the Public, chapter 1.)

Cleveland Bonsai Club

(meets at The Garden Center of Greater Cleveland at 7 p.m. on the 4th Wednesday of most months; annual membership fee: $15; monthly newsletter; contact Garden Center, 721-1600)

This club is restricted to 100 members who are practicing the Oriental art of bonsai (growing trees in shallow containers). "In the creation of bonsai, there are aesthetic principles which must be taken into consideration. Tree and container must be compatible as to size and shape and color; the tree itself must adhere to certain rules of proportion; it should appear as it does in nature but in miniature. By careful pruning and trimming, the tree is shaped to show its own essential beauty, to bring into harmony its trunk, branches and foliage," Club literature explains.

The Cleveland Bonsai Club was founded in 1956 by the late Viola Briner, librarian at The Garden Center, and Arthur Leudy, Cleveland nurseryman. Meetings are devoted to advice on potting, pruning, and general care plus practice sessions and demonstrations by recognized authorities.

Cleveland Cultural Garden Federation

(meets usually on the 2nd Tuesday of the month at 2 p.m. at Cleveland City Hall mayor's office or dining room; no annual membership fee; contact Alfonso D'Emilia, president, 932-2482)

The Cleveland Cultural Gardens Federation is a working group that interfaces between the city of Cleveland and the ethnic groups represented in the Cultural Gardens. An associate member of University Circle Incorporated, the federation includes about twenty delegates and their substitutes. But D'Emilia says anyone interested in the Cultural Gardens is welcome to attend the meetings and contribute to their efforts to raise money, maintain the gardens, and preserve the cultural heritage that the gardens reflect. The federation also works with newly organized ethnic groups who want to apply to put in their own cultural gardens.

Cleveland Ikenobo Society

(lessons twice a month on Saturday mornings from March to November in Parma; annual membership fee: $18; each lesson is $3 plus materials; contact Dorothy Kansaki, 888-3482)

This 30-member, ten-year-old chapter of the oldest school of Ikebana (Japanese flower arranging) is devoted to teaching the Ikenobo methods. The society also hosts workshops with internationally known instructors and holds public displays twice a year. The school's forty-fifth headmaster, Senei Ikenobo, who is headquartered in Kyoto, Japan, explains the school's background in a society brochure: "We try to arrange so there is harmony between the arranger and the plants—so the arrangement is in harmony with the environment."

Cleveland Rose Society

(meets on the 2nd Wednesday of most months, 7:30 p.m. at The Garden Center of Greater Cleveland; annual membership fees: $10 per family; monthly newsletter The Thorn; *[*The Rose, *a monthly magazine of the American Rose Society, is available with ARS membership]; contact Jim Wickert, 696-5729)*

This 150-member society was founded in 1932; members have been planting roses and consulting ever since. The society brings in internationally known speakers and has two annual rose shows. They host garden tours, lectures, and guest speakers of all kinds related to rose growing; they also demonstrate rose growing and pruning at The Garden Center's Rose Garden (see Gardens Open to the Public, chapter 1). Members who belong to the American Rose Society and like to share information can earn the rank of ARS consulting rosarians; those who show successfully can be trained as ARS judges.

(See also: Home and Garden Tours, chapter 2.)

Other rose societies have similar programs but concentrate their activities in different parts of Cleveland and the surrounding areas. They include:

- Akron Rose Society; contact Bob Choate, 235-2751
- Euclid Rose Society; contact Cal Schroeck, 585-0506
- Forest City Rose Society (a predominately west-side group); contact Bob Choate, 235-2751
- Northeast Ohio Rose Society (serves the Lake County Area; contact Ray Wickert, 428-2929

• Parma Rose Society (mostly south side); contact Helen Purcell, 251-3057

Dahlia Society of Ohio

(meets on the 1st Friday of most months, 7:30 p.m. at The Garden Center; annual membership fee: $7; Dahlia Digest monthly newsletter; contact Monica Rini, 461-4190)

The Dahlia Society is composed of people devoted to growing this wonderfully diverse class of native American tubers—with flowers ranging in size from half dollars to dinner plates in every color but blue. Just as there are a lot of dahlias available, there are a lot of people who grow them locally. Overall, the society has 150 members, making it larger than any other dahlia society in the Midwest (partly because it attracts dahlia enthusiast members from neighboring cities and states).

"People often join societies outside of their own region to get the newsletters and show announcements," said Monica Rini, 1992 president. "They also join ours because we give outstanding prizes at our shows."

The Dahlia Society holds a large dahlia show at a shopping mall in late summer and a second smaller show at The Garden Center on the first weekend in October. Many members also exhibit their flowers at the Cuyahoga and Geauga County fairs. Besides showing what they grow, the society holds auctions of dahlia tubers, hosts a July picnic and an August garden tour, operates a lending library of dahlia videos and books, and sells dahlias at The Garden Center's spring plant sale. Dahlia Society members are available to lecture to other groups.

(See also: Home and Garden Tours, chapter 2.)

Greater Cleveland Orchid Society

(meets one evening a month, usually at a restaurant; annual membership fee: $10 single, $12.50 family; monthly newsletter; contact Glen Sobola, 641-0206)

The Greater Cleveland Orchid Society, a group that's about fifty years old and 170 members strong, is concentrated on the east side of town. Their meetings usually include a well-known speaker—some nationally and internationally prominent—who talks about a certain kind of orchid and who often sells plants. They sometimes bring in top speakers for combined meetings with other local orchid groups. In August, the meetings adjourn for a summer picnic and plant auction. In spring, the club puts on a plant show at The Garden Center. Members can borrow from the club's small library of orchid books and videos.

Ikebana International, Cleveland Chapter 20

(meets on the 1st Wednesday of several months, during the daytime; annual membership fees: about $45; for information, contact The Garden Center, 721-1600)

Ikebana International, headquartered in Tokyo, Japan, is a worldwide group that includes the many schools of Japanese flower arranging. The group's goal is to encourage friendship through the study of flower arranging and other cultural arts of Japan. The Cleveland Chapter, founded in 1959, includes primarily the Ohara, Sogetsu, and Ikenobo styles of arranging, each of which has a structured curriculum and ranks of achievement (rather like the belt system in karate). The group has workshops from different Ikebana schools, annual public demonstrations, and internationally known speakers.

Ikebana International members also created, financed, and continue to support the Japanese Garden at The Garden Center (see chapter 1); they also organize periodic festivals.

Ichiyo School of Ikebana

(monthly group lessons on the 2nd Monday of each month at Community Center of Highland Heights; fees vary; contact Louise Taylor, master, 442-6769)

Students of the Ichiyo School of Ikebana use imagination to develop creative designs that reflect the nature of the designer, working through a simplified, but still structured, lesson program. Ichiyo is the only school of Ikebana to offer a correspondence course.

Indoor Gardening Society of America, Cleveland Chapter

(meets on the 4th Monday of most months, 7:30 p.m. at The Garden Center; annual membership fee: $5; monthly newsletter; contact Jack Keller, 382-8561)

The 110-member Indoor Gardening Society is devoted to exchanging ideas, methods, and experiences related to growing plants indoors. Meetings include local speakers, book reviews, demonstrations, and occasional nationally known experts for a special Sunday lecture. In October and March, the society holds Sunday plant sales.

"It's a great group—we all get a big kick out of putting on the two plant sales. Members donate all the plants, and we all work together for two days. Beyond that, the holiday party is a knock-out. We fill up the Duncan Room with about sixty festive people," said Jack Keller, a 10-year member who has five floral carts full of plants at his home.

The society also encourages indoor gardening by leasing floral light carts (at no charge) to nonprofit groups and giving scholarship grants to students of indoor gardening or making donations to the Cuyahoga Soil and Water Conservation District's forestry camp program.

Midwest Cactus and Succulent Society

(meets at members' homes on the 3rd Sunday of each month; annual membership fees: $5; contact Penny Chaikin, 381-2515)

This 60-year-old society of approximately thirty members sponsors potluck dinners and programs about cacti and succulents, shares slides, and holds a show and sale (usually on the first Sunday of March at The Garden Center). Several members have greenhouses but most grow cacti and succulents on windowsills or in light gardens.

The Midwest society is affiliated with the Cactus and Succulent Society of America, which is devoted to studying and appreciating this unusual group of plants. Membership in the national group ($35) gives access to the seeds of rare plants, field trips to exotic places, show-judge training, and a subscription to the bimonthly *Cactus and Succulent Society Journal*, a scholarly research and reference resource.

"Cactus and succulent societies are especially big in Germany, Britain, and many of the Slavic countries," said Penny Chaikin, local secretary/treasurer and national liaison. "You really don't know how many people are involved in these areas worldwide until you join a club. Last year, the national conference brought succulent growers from Europe, Japan, and Madagascar. It's just fantastic," Chaikin said.

Native Plant Society of Northeastern Ohio

(meets on varying weekends and evenings; annual membership fee: $10 active, $15 family, lifetime memberships available; On the Fringe quarterly magazine; contact Tom Sampliner, 321-3702)

This plant society was formed by a handful of people who attended a 1982 wildflower symposium held at the Holden Arboretum. The group now has about a hundred members. Its name reflects this society's broad range of interests, which include native trees, grasses, flowers, ferns and fern allies, mosses and liverworts, fungi, lichens, and algae. (Native plants are separated from more recent introductions by the fact that they were growing in Ohio at the time of European settlement.)

The group may canoe an isolated lake identifying plants, learn to propagate wildflowers and ferns or to identify plants in winter, and they sometimes hear local and national speakers. The monthly meeting dates vary: many are weekend field trips that range across northeast Ohio; some are lectures on weekday evenings. The group also plants wildflower gardens at the Cuyahoga County Library in Chagrin Falls and assists with the wildflower garden at The Garden Center.

"Our members include professional biologists and interested lay people—anyone who wants to see rare plants or wildflower gardens. I notice on our field trips that some of us are more partial to flowering plants, like carnivorous pitcher plants, wild orchids and gentians, but as long as we find something that is rare and endangered—flowering or not—it's pretty exciting," said Tom Sampliner, president.

Like the interesting programs, their *On the Fringe* newsletter includes club notices and informative articles, like what you might find in a winter walk through a bog or how society members plant and maintain Metropark's wildflower gardens.

Northern Ohio Perennial Society

(meets 4 times a year on the last Monday of the month, 7:30 p.m. at The Garden Center; annual membership fees: $10 for Garden Center members, $12 for non-Garden Center members; monthly newsletter in season; contact Eva Sands, 371-3363, or Betty McRainey, 732-9155)

The Northern Ohio Perennial Society began about eight years ago when founder Eva Sands organized a perennial swapping group. It has grown into an active society sponsoring lectures, information sharing, and garden tours. The society designs and maintains two perennial beds at The Garden Center.

"We love perennials because with them we know the joy of witnessing the rebirth of nature year after year. What gives more pleasure each spring than recognizing and welcoming each little familiar shoot as it valiantly reappears, having survived even the severest of winters," writes Sands.

This society also has sponsored publication of a new handbook, *Growing Perennials in Northern Ohio: Gardener to Gardener* (available from Dorothy Bier, 2672 Derbyshire Road, Cleveland Heights, 44106). "These are all perennials we have grown, so we know they are hardy and do well here. We give examples of ways to use and combine these perennials," said Bier, 1992 president.

Ohara School of Ikebana, Northern Ohio Chapter

(meets on Fridays during the day, approx. 5 months each year; contact The Garden Center, 721-1600)

This is a contemporary school of Ikebana that is intimately inspired by nature. The Ohara School uses traditional Ikebana containers and shallow bowls or containers designed by Unshin Ohara, founder of the Ohara School in the late 1800s. This alternative container expanded the possibilities for different classes of arrangements and for the use of different flowers.

Workshops are given by local teachers and occasionally by international masters. Many members also study Ikebana from one of several local masters.

Sogetsu School of Ikebana

(lessons held in varying locations, primarily west side; no annual membership fee; class fees vary; contact Reiko Nakajima 235-4324)

Considered a freer form than other Ikebana schools, the

Sogetsu School of Ikebana believes, according to club literature, that: "Anyone can arrange Ikebana anywhere, and with anything. It should be part of a lifestyle to be appreciated by many people from all over the world, rather than being considered just an exclusive aspect of Japanese culture to be enjoyed by a limited number of people. There are no limitations or strict regulations for remaining in a basic or patternized form for arranging flowers. A variety of flower arrangements is expected naturally—according to materials, the seasons and the individual."

Oldest Stone House Herb Society
(meets on the 4th Monday of every month, 7:30 p.m. at the Oldest Stone House, Lakewood; annual membership fee: $10 to join the Lakewood Historic Society plus $5 for the Herb Society; contact Karen Ita, 521-8503 evenings)

This is one of the newest local plant societies, developed to maintain the herb garden at Lakewood's Oldest Stone House and to promote interest and knowledge of herbs. The group has workshops and lectures plus meetings devoted to using herbs. They also maintain the Oldest Stone House Herb Garden.

(See also: Gardens Open to the Public, chapter 1.)

West Shore Arrangers
(meets on the 1st Tuesday of the month, mornings,; annual membership fees: $15; contact The Garden Center, 721-1600.)

This group, limited to 35 members, is devoted strictly to studying flower arranging, following the system given in the *Handbook of National Council of State Garden Clubs*. Members design and critique flower arrangements and give programs on this artistic process to other groups. Prospective new members must demonstrate flower-arranging abilities and apply for future membership openings.

West Shore Orchid Society

(meets on the 3rd Wednesday of every other month, evenings, at restaurants; annual membership fee: $10 per couple; newsletter; contact Mary McAtee, 166 Carolyn Dr., Elyria, 44039)

This is a west-side group of 116 members devoted to growing orchids. The society originated in 1945 and includes some folks who have been members for ten or more years. Many have greenhouses; a few grow orchids in light gardens. Meetings include lectures or slide shows featuring different kinds of orchids or different aspects of orchid growing. The group usually has a fall show or occasional orchid seminar with prominent national speakers.

Western Reserve Herb Society

(meets several Wednesdays each month in varying locations; annual membership fee: $45 active; $50 associate; monthly newsletter; contact The Garden Center of Greater Cleveland, 721-1600)

This 125-member organization recently celebrated its fiftieth anniversary. Its members have created a world-class herb garden and raised public consciousness about herbs through an annual herb fair and regular programs and activities.

They meet several times a month, with unit meetings for business and speakers; other regular monthly meetings focus on using herbs in cuisine or horticulture. During the growing season, many more work meetings are devoted to harvesting and blending herbal creations that are sold in the October fund-raising herb fair. In addition, many members meet on Tuesday and Thursday mornings to maintain the garden.

"Come down to the Garden on Tuesdays and you will be greeted with open arms," said Jean Ingalls, membership chairman. "That's how we get most of our members. In the Herb Society, there are lots of ways to express your own skills and interests. It is frowned upon to sit on your hands and only come to meetings. People are very ambitious about learning and disseminating information. And they are very generous in providing scholarship funds for horticulture students."

The society publishes a series of herbal handbooks and cookbooks, including new booklets: *Thyme* ($6.00) and *Herbs and Children* ($4.00)—both available (add 75 cents postage) if you write to Western Reserve Herb Society, 11030 East Boulevard, Cleveland 44106. The Society also publishes cookbooks, including *Cooking with Herb Scents* ($16.95 plus $2.50 postage and handling) and *Herbs: A Cookbook and More* ($7.50 plus $2.00 postage and handling)

Prospective members must have two sponsors who are active members, and they must attend a certain number of meetings to be considered for the membership openings that come up every year. When active, a member must attend six meetings a year.

(See also: The Garden Center entry in Gardens Open to the Public, chapter 1; Special Events, chapter 2.)

Finding a Garden Club

In addition to the many plant societies, there are hundreds of garden clubs in our area. Some are devoted to younger or older women, a few are just for men, and some attract people from certain communities. Some are devoted exclusively to gardening or flower arranging; others expand into home, fashion, and related fields. Some meet in the day; fewer meet in the evening. Some are affiliated with the Garden Club of Ohio; others are associated with the National Council of State Garden Clubs.

You can find out a bit about many garden clubs by calling The Garden Center of Greater Cleveland (721-1600), which keeps a list of over seventy garden clubs that are affiliated (a percentage of the club membership are members of The Garden Center, so they are entitled to use the meeting rooms).

But there are other groups that are not affiliated and prefer to meet in homes, libraries, or town halls. You can find out about them by asking around your neighborhood, looking in the meeting section of your community newspaper, finding out who is planting flowers in community centers or village squares (which your mayor's office or chamber of commerce would know), or attending flower shows at nearby malls.

Plant Shows: What Are They? What Do They Mean?

Plant societies often stage shows of their best plants or cut flowers; flower arrangers may display arrangements that fit a certain theme. Whether the shows are exhibitionary or judged, they provide a chance for the group to show off what they can do and a chance for you to see the best specimens, be it orchids or Ikebana arrangements. You can read about fabulous flowers all you want, but their beauty will not be as real to you as if you see them in person.

The Rose Society and Dahlia Society members exhibit cut flowers—each carefully labeled—hoping to earn a ribbon or trophy. In these kinds of shows, flowers are judged according to very specific criteria established by the national organization. A prize winner is an example of perfection; it doesn't necessarily mean that the plant is easy to grow or is good for using in the landscape. If you see a flower you cannot live without in your own garden, take the time to learn the ins and outs of growing it from society members who are manning the show.

Other societies, such as the Bonsai Club and Ikebana International, display their plants in a noncompetitive fashion. Think of these displays as works of art; stand back and admire the concepts, shapes, colors, and combinations. You may someday become so entranced that you will decide to take up these avocations.

CHAPTER FIVE

❧

Understanding Our Natural Resources

WHETHER YOU ARE AN experienced gardener or a novice, it is important to understand the natural resources that affect your garden in so many ways. Any growing plant is intimately tied to soil and sun, rain and snow, wind, humidity, temperature—all of which together provide the substances it needs to grow. When you understand what to expect from weather and earth you can then make better decisions about what, how, when, and where to plant.

Certain generalizations can be made about our region's natural resources that usually prove true. But climate and soil can also vary widely from site to site within the region, and for numerous reasons. The following sections discuss the climate of greater Cleveland and the great variety of weather it brings, and the region's primary soil types and what they mean for gardeners.

CLIMATE

Northeast Ohio Climate: Expect the Unexpected

Each time the weather does what we don't expect, many gardeners are surprised, However, history says we should be learning to expect the unexpected. An 1863 letter mentioned in *Western Reserve Magazine* describes weather fluctuations that fell upon an early Cleveland Shaker farming community: "Ever since the fore part of April way into June it was so wet and cold in these parts that nothing would grow, especially in this stiff clay." The same article also mentions "Droughts [no rain for months in 1851] and late frosts [ice a quarter inch thick on June 9, 1862]." Does some of this sound familiar?

As with any hobby that is tied to nature, conditions for gardening vary—from week to week, season to season, decade to decade. Contemporary Clevelanders need go no further than to compare the summers of 1991 and 1992: 1991 featured a heavy drought; 1992 was drenched with excessive rain. The last spring frost in 1991 was in April; in 1992 it came at the end of May and almost made a repeat performance in June. Recent winters, too, have been quite different: 1990 featured low temperatures in the sub-zero range (our usual); 1991 rarely saw a dip below the teens. Dealing effectively with climate can be one of the principal challenges for gardeners.

What Is Climate?

Climate is the prevailing set of natural conditions that affect a particular region—the noticeable and measurable features that make us (and our plants) hot or cold, soggy or dehydrated, and, in some cases, alive or dead. These features include temperature, precipitation (rain, sleet, hail, snow), humidity, sunlight, wind. In addition, climate includes the more or less consistent patterns of seasonal change that a region experiences. Local climate is largely a product of wider, even global, climate patterns interacting with regional variations in topography (the natural and man-made features of the landscape). Within even local climates there is room for further regional variation.

Local Climate

Ours is a region on the edge. The greater Cleveland area straddles three different geographic sections: we are bounded on the north by Lake Erie, on the south and east by the western edge the glaciated Allegheny Plateau, and on the west and northwest by the Eastern Lake and Till Plains.

Our terrain is generally level, with the exception of the east side's "heights," actually a single large ridge rising about five hundred feet above shore level. Other principal geographic features are the Cuyahoga, Chagrin, and Rocky rivers—the area's principal drainage into Lake Erie. These rivers create valleys 100 to 150 feet below the surrounding land surface.

Our climate has been described as generally "continental" in character—moderately warm summers and relatively cold winters with abundant, though varying, precipitation. But the strong modifying influence of Lake Erie gives our climate's character its own special twist.

On the U.S. Department of Agriculture's hardiness map, most of northeast Ohio is classified within zone 5, with sections fronting the lake included in zone 6. (You'll find hardiness zones listed in many gardening books and catalogues. It's good to remember your zone so you can choose plants accordingly.) Various factors, however, make the greater Cleveland area different from even nearby areas classified in the same zones. For example, central Ohio is also in zone 5, but we tend to get more cloud cover in winter than they do; that cloudiness keeps our daytime high temperatures lower, because the sun doesn't get through to warm up the air below. Our zone 6 areas also tend to have cooler summers than southern Ohio's zone 6.

Proximity to Lake Erie, which moderates summer and winter temperatures for those within a couple of miles of its shore, is partly responsible for this difference. It also produces lake effect snows on the east and south sides that are unpredictable—and unusual, as well. In fact, according to TV8 weatherman Dick Goddard (as quoted in *The Plain Dealer*), such lake effect snows happen in only four locations worldwide: "The southeast shorelines of the Great Lakes and Hudson Bay, Canada; the eastern side of Great Salt Lake, Utah, and the Japanese island of Hokkaido." These are the only places where winds can sweep across an expanse of unfrozen water, picking up moisture, then move directly onto the colder shore where the moisture will fall as snow.

Even within the borders of Cuyahoga County there are significant geographic and climatic differences; the west side varies from the east, the east from the south, and all differ from the lake shore. These make up microclimates (differences in exposure, moisture, sun, and other factors that alter conditions for plant growth). Some of this region's major climatic variations that most affect gardeners are detailed here:

Lake Effect

Complex conditions that we call the "lake effect" cause this area to have milder weather. Because large bodies of water take a long time to warm up, spring can be cooler very near the lake. "On those warm spring afternoons in April and early May, when baseball first begins, it can be 75° or 80°F at the airport but 55° or 60°F downtown because the lake water is about 55°F. This cooling trend stays near the lake unless there are strong northerly winds," said Alan Ringo, National Weather Service hydrologist.

The Garden Center of Greater Cleveland (about two and a half miles from the lake) benefits from milder fall weather courtesy of Lake Erie; the water takes longer to cool in fall, and so keeps nearby areas warmer, often delaying the first frost and moderating winter low temperatures. Alexander Apanius, director of The Garden Center, explained, "The lake keeps cold air from descending near the plants . . . so we can grow plants like umbrella pine (*Sciadopitys verticillata*), Japanese cryptomeria (*Cryptomeria japonica*), Japanese snowball (*Styrax japonicus*), and Franklin tree (*Franklinia alatamaha*) that would not do well in flat open areas away from the lake." At the Rockefeller Park Greenhouse, myrtles, big-leaf magnolias, and albizzias surprisingly survive.

The lake also releases moisture into the air that often is taken eastward by prevailing winds. When the moist air hits the higher-altitude areas from Chardon to Bainbridge, the moisture falls as rain or snow. One benefit of this effect: because snow cover insulates plants that are dormant in the ground, marginally hardy plants have a better chance of survival where snowfall is heavier.

The lake effect snows concentrate on the south and east parts of the region. The west side, according to meteorologist Fred Johnson, is spared because the winds tend to run parallel with the shore line there and because it has slightly less elevation.

Rainfall Exceptions

Amount of rainfall can vary significantly between the east and west sides of Cleveland. Like lake effect snows in winter, lake effect rains are caused by moisture rising off the lake, moving east in the prevailing winds, hitting the eastern highlands, rising, cooling, and then dropping as rain. During a 1934 drought, a Cleveland Museum of Natural History researcher calculated that 22.8 inches of rain fell in downtown Cleveland while 39.2 inches fell 15 miles away in the North Chagrin Metropark reservation.

There are occasional variations in this general rainfall pattern, though, because our weather comes from many directions. For instance, in the wet summer of July, 1992, *The Plain Dealer* reported 9.25 inches of rain fell in Parma, the peak area for the month, and close to 7 inches fell across most of West-lake, Olmsted Township, and Strongsville; 8.25 inches fell in Moreland Hills and only 4.25 in Mayfield Heights.

Shelter in the City

Because there is more pavement reflecting heat and more buildings to cut cold winds, city dwellers tend to have milder winters and earlier springs. I have a friend who lives near I-77 in the heart of the city. Every year, he plants his corn in late April or early May—earlier than is normal for this area—but he gets away with it because he gardens in the warmer city zone.

The concentration of buildings in the city also provides more shade than might be accounted for in a general projection for this zone. Local shade patterns can make it difficult to grow sun-loving plants, including common flowers (like roses and geraniums) and vegetables (such as tomatoes and peppers). Similar circumstances occur in the older suburbs, where large old shade trees block the sun. Wherever you garden, count the hours of sun on the site (which will vary during the course of the year): sun-loving plants need six hours or more of sunlight; more shade-tolerant plants usually require four hours. Note that buildings can reflect sun as well as block it; gardens planted near south-facing walls can experience hotter and drier conditions than on other sides of the same building.

The urban landscape affects city gardeners' soil, too, which often stays drier because rainfall is channeled from pavement directly into sewers without moving through the soil.

Slope

Slope is the angle of a land surface (generally measured as a percentage of vertical drop over horizontal distance). Although slope effects may not make dramatic differences in how your plants grow, you will find that plants on slopes facing different directions start growing or blooming at different times. Slopes facing south receive the most sun, so they warm sooner in spring. North-facing slopes have the least sun, so they warm more slowly. Slopes facing east warm slightly sooner than north, because they will receive cool morning sun. Slopes facing west will warm slightly sooner than east, because they receive the warm afternoon sun.

Cool air also collects at the bottom of a slope, sometimes sparing plants higher up on the hill from severe cold or hard frosts. "In one of our outlying collections a true cedar, which is marginally hardy, survives unattended," said Jim Mack, superintendant of the Holden Arboretum grounds. "It's growing on the upper half of a slope, away from where cold air is dumped, and nestled amid other plants that cut the wind."

Climate Statistics

Here are some specific weather data that further describe the Cleveland area climate, and which may help you plan your gardening around the elements:

• Frost-free Growing Season

Our average frost-free growing season runs about 160 days, although it can be a month longer near the lakeshore.

Probability of a freeze:

before		after	
Oct 8:	10%	April 30:	50%
Oct 13:	20%	May 13:	20%
Oct 23:	50%	May 20:	10%

"Determining the date for first frost in fall and the last frost in spring is almost a guessing game," said Jack Kerrigan, Cuyahoga County Cooperative Extension agent. "The data the Extension Service provides on the timing of frosts is only an average and mean. You need to look at the extremes, the historical highs and lows for any given day, too. For instance, although we say the first fall frost usually comes around October 15, it has been much later for the past few years."

- *Temperature*
  - The lowest temperature on record is -19°F (January 1963).
  - The highest recorded temperature is 104°F (June 1988).
  - The average annual soil temperature is about 2°F higher than the average annual air temperature.
  (See table of temperature data in this section.)

- *Precipitation*
  - Total precipitation (rain, snow, hail, etc., measured in water equivalents) averages 35 inches a year, but two years in ten will have less than 30 inches or more than 40 inches.
  - Usually 60 percent, or 20 inches, of our rainfall comes between April and September. During two years out of any ten, however, it can fall below 16 inches.
  - Snowfall averages 53 inches a year. About 28 days per winter we have one inch of snow on the ground.
  (See table of precipitation data in this section.)

- *Wind*
  - The prevailing, or most frequent, wind blows from the south and southwest.
  - Monthly average wind speeds range only slightly from 8.3 m.p.h. in August to 12 m.p.h. in December through March.

Climate Data

Precipitation

Precipitation Average in water equivalent inches, period of record (1871–1991)

Jan	Feb	Mar	Apr	May	Jun	Jul	Aug	Sep	Oct	Nov	Dec	Annual
2.5	2.3	2.9	2.9	3.2	3.4	3.4	3.1	3.2	2.6	2.7	2.6	34.7

Precipitation Average, water equivalent inches, last five years

	Jan	Feb	Mar	Apr	May	Jun	Jul	Aug	Sep	Oct	Nov	Dec	Annual
1988	1.0	2.8	2.2	3.5	1.3	0.7	3.4	3.4	1.8	2.5	4.6	2.5	29.7
1989	2.1	1.7	3.5	3.7	9.1	5.2	3.0	1.1	4.6	4.5	3.6	1.7	43.9
1990	2.4	4.7	0.9	4.6	6.1	1.7	5.6	4.8	7.3	4.9	2.3	8.6	53.8
1991	2.2	2.3	3.6	4.2	3.2	1.4	1.7	2.8	3.4	2.7	2.9	2.3	32.7
1992	3.3	2.7	3.1	3.8	3.0	2.7	9.1	4.6	3.3	2.3	6.5	4.3	48.5
5-yr.	2.2	2.8	2.6	4.0	4.6	2.3	4.6	3.3	4.1	3.4	4.0	3.9	41.7

Cloud Cover

Normal Number of Days, sunrise to sunset that are:

	Jan	Feb	Mar	Apr	May	Jun	Jul	Aug	Sep	Oct	Nov	Dec	Annual
Clear	3	3	4	5	6	7	9	9	8	8	3	3	67
Ply Cldy	5	6	7	8	10	11	12	11	10	8	6	5	97
Cloudy	23	20	20	17	15	12	11	11	12	15	21	24	201

(Above data from *Local Climatological Data* for Cleveland, Ohio, National Oceanic and Atmospheric Administration)

Climate Data

Temperature

Temperature Averages °F, period of record (1871–1991)

	Jan	Feb	Mar	Apr	May	Jun	Jul	Aug	Sep	Oct	Nov	Dec	Annual
Avg.													
High	34	35	44	56	67	77	81	79	73	62	49	38	58
Low	20	20	28	39	49	59	64	62	56	45	35	25	42
Mean	27	28	36	47	58	68	72	71	65	54	42	31	50

Normal Average Temperatures °F (data from comparison period 1951–1980)

	Jan	Feb	Mar	Apr	May	Jun	Jul	Aug	Sep	Oct	Nov	Dec	Annual
Avg.													
High	33	35	45	58	69	78	82	80	74	63	49	38	59
Low	19	20	28	38	48	57	61	61	54	44	34	25	41
Mean	26	27	37	48	58	68	72	70	64	53	42	31	50

Record Temperatures

	Jan	Feb	Mar	Apr	May	Jun	Jul	Aug	Sep	Oct	Nov	Dec	Annual
High	73	69	83	88	92	104	103	102	101	90	82	77	104
Low	-19	-15	-5	10	25	31	41	38	32	19	3	-15	-19

(Above data from Local Climatological Data for Cleveland, Ohio, National Oceanic and Atmospheric Administration)

Local Climatological Data

Certain climate statistics collected by the National Weather Service are published by the National Oceanic and Atmospheric Administration in a periodical titled *Local Climatological Data* (LCD). Monthly and annual summaries for Cleveland, Akron, and Youngstown are available by mail from:

National Climatic Data Center
Federal Building
37 Battery Park Avenue
Asheville, NC 28801-2733
704-259-0871

Subscriptions to these and other related periodicals are also available.

The local data collection site for the Cleveland area is:
National Weather Service Forecast Office
Cleveland Hopkins Airport
Cleveland, 44135
(216) 265-2370

Local all-weather radio is broadcast on 162.55 MHZ and 162.40 MHZ 24 hours a day.

TV8 Weatherline recorded message: 881-0880.

Dealing with Climate: Be Prepared

Your landscape, with the exception of the few lucky plants grown in movable containers, cannot escape these moody outdoor elements. Landscape plants will be exposed to the best and worst of our weather. For these plants to succeed despite such extremes, it's important to plan ahead for difficulties.

Raise planting beds several inches or more above ground level so that excess moisture can drain off. Plan a watering program so you can irrigate when the weather is dry. You can buy inexpensive soaker hoses or high-tech drip irrigation systems. Even save your gray water (the water that is left over from rinsing clothing or vegetables) for use on your plants. Protect tender plants with floating row covers (lightweight fabric draped over plants to keep them several degrees warmer than the surrounding air temperature and also to keep out flying pests). Or make your own light shade with horticultural shade cloth, a lath house, or a sun-blocking trellis to keep cool-season crops alive in unexpectedly hot weather. Look for cultivars that tolerate both hot and cool temperatures, such as newer weather-resistant pansies or multiflora petunias. You can find designs for raised beds, trellises, and similar garden projects in books such as *Wood Projects for the Garden* (by Ron Hildebrand, 1987, Ortho Books, San Francisco, CA).

Try to remain flexible and be willing to adapt your plans when the unforeseen inevitably comes. A late May frost, an unusually warm winter, or an excessively wet or dry month will affect your garden and landscape. Start a few tomatoes early in movable patio planters if early spring is mild. Bring them indoors, if you must, to escape a late storm.

Working with the weather is what makes gardening so much fun when a project succeeds, and such a challenge when a project progresses contrary to plans. Preparation helps, but flexibility is a necessity. Whether you grow a couple of pepper plants, a backyard of show dahlias, or a high-fashion landscape, northeast Ohio climate will continue to intrigue.

Soil

For gardeners, soil means the upper layer of earth that can be dug or plowed and in which plants grow. Soil types vary widely, because their many properties form over time in the complex interaction of minerals, organic matter, and effects of physical relief and climate (such as erosion and decomposition).

Basically, the soils of greater Cleveland were formed in the time since the last glaciers (about 10,000 to 15,000 years ago) and thus are characterized largely by glacial till, a mixture of gravel and clay dropped by the receding ice.

Since that time, a lot has happened to cause local variations. Plants and animals, their type and location determined in part by climate, decomposed with the help of microflora (earthworms, fungi, and bacteria and other microscopic creatures) to release nutrients into the soil. Some of those organic nutrients, along with minerals, washed away with streams and ground water and layered on top of other other soils. Patterns of water runoff and drainage also caused erosion, which lowered some surfaces nearer to bedrock (what was there before the glaciers), exposing them to different minerals. More recently, man has altered the soil by moving it from place to place and by adding fertilizers and other chemicals.

The result of all this is that the Cleveland area provides gardeners with several basic soil types and a wide variety of local variations.

A few generalizations can be made about our soils and their use for gardening:

• Most soils in this region are naturally acid. Acidity, which will influence the kinds of nutrients available to plants, is measured in pH. An acid soil is rated below neutral 7 on the pH scale, while an alkaline or basic soil, high in limestone, is rated above 7. Most plants grow well from pH 6.5 to 7. If your soil has a lower pH, you can add ground limestone to bring the pH higher. Effects of lime are temporary—based on the type of limestone and acidity of soil. If in a year or so your plants are yellowing or growing slowly, have the pH tested again.

• Most soils in this region are moderately low in organic matter. Compost, decayed livestock manure, or peat moss will generally benefit the growing of flowers and vegetables.

• Most Cleveland-area gardeners also struggle with heavy clay soils, which hold water, stay cool and soupy longer in spring, and rot plant roots if you don't provide a route for drainage.

However, a few locations around northeast Ohio have light sandy loams, a welcome relief from clay. West of Euclid and east of downtown, a two- to three-mile-wide, 28-mile-long strip along Lake Erie's shoreline was once occupied by glacial lakes. These lakes left sandy loams, ideal for growing plants. You can see how well these soils grow plants by visiting The Garden Center or the Rockefeller Park Greenhouse, both of which are blessed with these soils. Similar sandy ridges left by sand dunes or lake beds extend inland west from the Cuyahoga River near Schaaf Road (once a thriving farming area), Detroit Avenue, Triskett, and Hilliard. This soil is also found along Middle Ridge Road in Lake County, an area with many nurseries.

Cleveland's west side, predominately gray clay, is less prone to developing large swampy areas than the east side (although most such swamps are now drained). It tends to be better drained than the east side because it slopes gradually down to the Cuyahoga River Valley.

Beyond these generalizations, it's extremely difficult to discuss the Cleveland-area soil in specific terms, because it can change significantly almost from backyard to backyard. Local soils offer different combinations of minerals and organic matter, consistency, drainage, and aeration to challenge gardeners.

But there is an excellent way for gardeners to find out exactly what's in *their* soil.

Start with the *Soil Survey of Cuyahoga County, Ohio*, a large book of soil maps published by the U.S. Department of Agriculture and the Ohio Department of Natural Resources. The *Soil Survey* gives precise locations of hundreds of soil types found throughout the county. You can pinpoint your own home on aerial photo maps and find out exactly what the name of your soil type is, then call either department to get an explanation of what that soil type means for your garden.

The *Soil Survey* is available free from the county Soil and Water Conservation District offices of the U.S. Department of Agriculture (Cuyahoga: 524-6580, Geauga: 834-1122, Lake: 357-2730, Lorain: 322-1228, Medina: 722-2605, Portage: 296-4311, Summit: 929-2871) or the County Cooperative Extension Service (Cuyahoga: 631-1890, Geauga: 834-4656, Lake: 357-2582, Lorain: 322-0127, Medina: 725-4911, Summit: 497-1611).

However, in most of the urban areas of Cleveland the *Soil Survey* map's use may be limited, says James Storer, of the U.S. Department of Agriculture's Soil Conservation Service.

"In urban areas, often the topsoil has been removed or compacted, or fill dirt has been brought in from other places and layered on top of the existing soil. The soil you have now may not be anything like what was originally there." In the outlying suburbs, such as Bay Village, Westlake, Olmsted Township, Strongsville, Broadview Heights, Solon, and Gates Mills, though, the map remains pretty accurate.

You can run a few simple tests on your soil to verify what the *Soil Survey* reports. To figure out if your soil is clay, squeeze a handful of soil about two days after a rainfall. If the handful of soil stays molded in a ball or if you can squeeze it out into a long ribbon, you have clay. If you have a sandy loam, the handful of soil will break up instead of clinging tightly in a ball or a ribbon.

And you can have nutrient levels in your soil tested by the Cooperative Extension Service for a small fee. Call the county office near you and have them send you a test package.(See phone numbers listed above.)

For more information on soil preparation, look at *The Rodale Book of Composting* (edited by Grace Gershuny and Deborah Martin, 1992, Rodale Press, Emmaus, PA).

NATIVE AND WILD PLANTS OF OUR REGION

In addition to knowing your local climate and soil, it's helpful to be familiar with the region's naturally occurring vegetation. If there are no woodlands in your neighborhood, use the nearest Metropark reservation or local nature center. Walk around with an identification guide and check out what species are

growing in situations similar to your own landscape. One good such guide is: *A Field Guide to Trees & Shrubs: Northeast and North Central U.S. and Southeast and South Central Canada*, Peterson Guide Series (by George Petrides, 1986, Houghton, Mifflin, Boston, MA).

In more undisturbed rural areas, you can find oaks and hickories growing in drier terrain, including the Brecksville Reservation; beach and maple trees enjoy moister soils on the eastern side of town. Northern species such as yellow birch, Canadian hemlocks, and Canadian yew remain in the cooler ravines of the Metroparks, and white pines grow on the top of 1,300-foot-high Little Mountain in Lake County. Elsewhere, these plants perished as our climate warmed some four thousand years ago and new species—including tulip, poplar, magnolia, hickories, black walnut, red mulberry, sassafras, shadbush, and rhododendron—moved in from the south.

Trees That Grow Naturally in Northeast Ohio

• In drier areas of the west side, you'll find white, red, and black oak, chinquapin oak, and shagbark and butternut hickory.

• In the western lake plain, look for beech, maple, tulip, white ash, tupelo, basswood, and white oak.

• Closer to the Cuyahoga Valley you will find more oaks and tulip trees. In the southern highlands, look for some white pine, hemlock, and yellow birch among the many beech and maple trees.

• The eastern part of greater Cleveland has species such as beech, maple, tulip trees, cucumber magnolia, tupelo, hop hornbeam, shadbush, witch hazel, and spicebush.

• In wetter areas, silver maple, pin oak, sycamore, and tupelo will grow.

Moses Cleaveland Trees

A good way to find a tree that will live for centuries is to find a nearby Moses Cleaveland tree. These trees are thought to be old enough to have been growing when Moses Cleaveland arrived in this area in 1796. Many are labeled with plaques; others are identified by location in the Moses Cleaveland tree records in city hall. As of 1984 (the most recent survey), over two hundred trees were documented in Cuyahoga County. Among them were a:

- White oak on the Baldwin-Wallace College campus in Berea, 44 inches in trunk diameter
- Black gum at The Garden Center, 32 inches
- White oak at Nela Park, Noble Road, East Cleveland, 40 inches
- White oak at Southwest General Health Care, Middleburg Heights, 58 inches
- White oak at Sunset Memorial Park, Olmsted Falls, 48 inches
- White oak at Grantwood Recreation Center, Solon, 47 inches
- Red oak at Evergreen Cemetery, Westlake, 64 inches

If you know of a tree that might qualify, call the City of Cleveland Tree Commission (664-3104); their foresters will inspect the tree. Once given their okay, the Early Settlers Association gives the tree a seal of approval. Do so before 1996, when these trees will become a prominent part of a meeting of the International Society of Arboriculture that will be held here.

Planting Considerations

Whether using native plants or some of the many plants from other parts of the world that also make excellent low-maintenance garden subjects, plan before planting. When you bring in species from different climates think carefully about how well they will adjust here. Some commonly grown landscape plants relocated here are suffering because our climate is not right for them. Colorado blue spruce and white birch trees, which come from cooler climates, are dying from cankers, borers, and miners. At fault, according to Roger Funk of Davey Tree Service, is not the plants but the climate. It simply has become too warm here for them to grow strongly enough to resist otherwise minor problems.

Another problem arises when Cleveland-area homeowners put species in sites where they cannot grow easily. Our native flowering dogwood, which normally grows beneath the light shade of a taller tree, when put in full sun in the middle of a lawn is more likely to suffer from insects and diseases. It is best set in the rich leaf humus and light shade at the edge of a woodland.

Native Wildflowers

Like trees, wildflowers grow in different habitats (environments made up of different soils, moisture levels, and light in which certain plants usually live). There are two general habitat types in our region: deciduous woodlands and prairies. There are also many variations in the particular site conditions and species found within these two habitats.

In the deciduous woodlands, especially those areas with large mature shade trees, you can find a rich flora of spring-blooming wildflowers. These perennial wildflowers flourish in dark, spongy soil that has been enriched for decades by the decay of autumn leaves. Most of these wildflowers emerge in early spring and bloom before the trees leaf out, peppering the woods with white flowers and occasional pink, blue, and yellow blossoms. Many of these species die back to dormant roots by summer.

If you are willing to build an organically rich soil beneath deeper rooted shade trees (many maples root so thickly near the soil surface that there is little space left for smaller plants), you may be able to start a self-perpetuating spring wildflower garden. You need to look into the specific moisture and light requirements of each species you plant, though—they do vary. Check with the Native Plant Society (see Plant Societies, chapter 4), Holden Arboretum, the Cleveland Museum of Natural History, or the Cleveland Metroparks (see Gardens Open to the Public, chapter 1). Or consult *The Wildflower Gardener's Guide: Northeast, Mid-Atlantic, Great Lakes, Eastern Canada* (by Henry Art, 1987, Storey Communications, Pownal, VT) or *Wildflowers* (by Rick Imes, 1992, Rodale Press, Emmaus, PA).

Some of our more notable spring wildflowers include: wild columbine, jack-in-the-pulpit, Virginia bluebells, Dutchman's-breeches, wild geraniums, violets, foamflower, bloodroot, Solomon's-seal, hepatica, trilliums, and trout lily. You can find some of these species propagated at several nurseries listed in the Specialty Growers section in chapter 3. You can also rescue wildflowers from construction sites, but please don't dig them from the woods (or buy from companies who take them from public woods). If everyone dug up a couple of woodland wildflowers, we would destroy this great natural resource. Unfortunately, our state wildflower, the large flowered trillium (*Trillium grandiflorum*), is quite difficult to propagate and may only be available from sources who collect it in natural areas.

Prairie wildflowers inhabit open fields, and sometimes roadsides, with full sun and drier soil. Prairie plants tend to bloom in summer and fall. Many can spread vigorously when conditions are right, which has led to their use in what many gardeners hope will be low-maintenance meadow gardens. Sometimes the meadow garden works; sometimes it does not. (See Using Wildflower Mixes Conscientiously in chapter 6.)

Some of the native American meadow and prairie species found locally include: purple coneflower, black-eyed Susan, prairie blazing-star, perennial sunflowers, goldenrods, New England asters, butterfly weed, and wild bergamot.

You'll also find plenty of wildflowers from other parts of the world growing locally, including Queen Anne's lace, oxeye daisy, common yarrow, and common chicory.

HISTORICAL HORTICULTURE
AND OUR OWN GARDENS

By looking at early cultivation of land in northeast Ohio, we can get some eye-opening revelations that apply to what we are still doing today. Although our landscape has changed dramatically from a woodland to an urban and suburban metropolis, we are still dealing with similar soils and climate, even though both have been altered somewhat by construction, soil compaction, pavement, and buildings.

Crops

The earliest crops grown in this area remain some of the most sure-fire to grow today. The Adena Indians grew pumpkins, squash, sunflowers, and corn. The first farmers in the Western Reserve area grew corn, vegetables, and apple trees. Medina opened into a great wheat- and corn-producing district. By 1840, farmers who happened to colonize near the Lake Erie shoreline learned of its superior sandy loam soil and moderate temperatures; they began to cultivate less hardy peaches, which they used for peach brandy, and the more temperamental types of grapes. Kelley's Island soon replaced Cincinnati as the biggest wine-producing area in the state.

The Shakers, a religious sect that settled in what is now Shaker Heights, were forward-thinking gardeners. In the mid-1800s, they practiced organic gardening techniques and fruit-tree culture that we consider modern; they also sold herbs by mail.

Soil Building

The Shakers found that organic methods of soil building were essential for raising crops in the stiff clay soils of this area. "No good farmer would consider starving his cattle and swine and expect them to produce; neither should he starve his land," wrote one Shaker farmer. They enriched the soil with barnyard manure, as some present-day gardeners do.

Another early diary advised: "For a really good corn crop, begin one year ahead. . . . First spread [livestock] dung on the sward; then plow deep and harrow thoroughly—then plant the whole field in potatoes. After the potatoes are dug in fall, drag into the land 15 to 20 ox-loads of barnyard manure to the acre; then plow it thoroughly. The next spring, after the harrowing, draw on 20 or more loads of green barn manure to the acre and let it lay for a few days. Just before planting, plow this in. This last coating will hold the moisture and bring corn to maturity in the last stages while the other coats mixed with the soil will start the corn with the greatest luxuriance in the early stages of its growth." (For more on this subject, see Making and Using Compost, chapter 6.)

The Shakers rotated crops (growing a succession of unrelated plants in any garden location to prevent the buildup of pests or diseases specific to particular crops and to avoid depleting certain nutrients by heavy-feeding crops). The

Shaker corn field was a good example of rotation. Potatoes, an underground crop, loosened the soil and did not consume large quantities of nutrients. In the season after the potatoes, the corn crop could develop deep roots and have an abundance of nutrients for good growth. In addition, the Shakers selected their own seed from superior corn plants, those with two or more ears per stalk, so they would get more food per plant.

Although the Shakers forbade ornamentation and luxury in their things, they did luxuriate in the same sense of peace that we modern gardeners enjoy when are absorbed in our gardens. A Shaker journal from June 1844 reads, "It is a perfect summer day. Not even a cloud disturbs the peace of the scene where out in the meadows the scyths of the brethren move in complete rhythm, while the sisters move quietly along the even kept rows, gathering berries and sweet smelling herbs in their well-kept gardens."

Herbs

The Shakers grew medicinal herbs for their own use and later expanded their gardens into a thriving mail-order business. It was to stock their community infirmaries that the Shakers began collecting the wild herbs of the New World, and it wasn't long before they had planted small physic gardens with imported seed of European medicinal plants. As the "outside world" (anyone who was not a Shaker) sampled the sect's herbs, demand grew. The herb gardens became larger, more varied, and more sophisticated.

When collecting herbs, the Shakers followed rigid rules set up to assure purity. Only one type of herb was picked at a time, and the harvest would be delivered to the processing area before the collection of a second herb was begun. In order to keep the herbs whole and undamaged, fragile plants were placed on 15-foot-square sheets; roots were placed in baskets. Plants were collected in season only: flowers as their buds opened or when in full bloom; berries when ripe; bark in spring, when the sap rose; roots when the plants had finished growing. Prime time for leafy plants was before the sun grew hot but after the dew dried. All of these points are good ideas, even today, if you harvest your own culinary herbs.

Fruit Trees

In 1840, Elijah Russell became head horticulturist for the local Shakers and began an aggressive fruit tree program. He planted orchards, experimented with new cultivars, grafted new forms onto existing trees, and fine-tuned pruning procedures. He wrote, "All trees in their growth seek to accomplish two things, the formation of wood and fruit buds. If too many wood buds are allowed to develop, very little fruit will mature. Pinch back the wood buds, trim apple trees from July onward; if trimmed in April or May they will bleed too freely, producing black cankers in the wound. Trimming in July and August will force the full strength of growth into the fruit buds."

Although Russell is right about thinning growth buds and fruit buds so the plant does not become overcrowded with branches or fruits, we now prune fruit trees primarily when they are dormant in early spring.

Another great early fruit specialist was Dr. Jared P. Kirtland. In 1840, he bought 83 acres of land between Detroit Road and Lake Erie. Kirtland found the climate near Lake Erie ideal but saw some fault with the soil. He believed, "The evil consists primarily in a deficient quantity of lime in the soil and . . . a deficiency also of animal and vegetable matter." In other words, the soil was too acidic and low in organic matter—manure and leaf compost.

In all, Kirtland developed 30 new varieties of cherries,

using an arduous technique. Collecting seed from his finest cherries, he grew the seedlings closely together so that they would hybridize. From the best 5,000 hybrid fruits on the first generation of trees, he would let only the most promising ten percent grow to maturity. And, of these, only one out of ten was deemed to be of any value. From a start of 5,000 trees, he was now down to 50 and, of these 50, only the very best would be selected for propagation by budding and grafting.

We think about an apple a day as a way to keep the doctor away. But early settlers in this area needed a bit of coaxing to enjoy both wild and early domesticated apples.

"The free use of ripe fruits not only prevents disease, but their regulated enjoyment helps to remove that which already exists. All ripe fruits are, also, more or less nutritious. Professor Salisbury has clearly demonstrated that the APPLE is superior to the POTATO in the principles that go to increase the muscle and brain of man," wrote F. R. Elliott, author of *The Western Fruit Book*, 1859.

Thomas Fessenden, author of the 1828 *New American Gardener*, writes: "Apples are thought to alter and ameliorate the taste and tone of the human system, in such a manner as to destroy that artificial appetite, which is gratified by the deleterious preparations of alcohol. 'The palate,' says Mr. Knight, a celebrated English horticulturist, 'which relishes fruit, is seldom pleased with strong fermented liquors; . . . supplying the public with fruit at a cheap rate would have a tendency to operate favourably, both on the physical and moral health of the people'. In medicine, verjuice, or the juice of crab apples, is used for sprains, and as an astringent and repellent. The good table apple, when ripe, is laxative; the juice is useful in dysenteries; boiled or roasted apples fortify a weak stomach."

For more information on tree pruning, see my book *All About Pruning* (1989, Ortho Books, San Francisco, CA) or *Fruits and Berries for the Home Garden* (by Lewis Hill, 1990, Garden Way Publishing, Pownal, VT).

Early Garden Detectives

Cleveland resident Connie White has been working to gather detailed information about turn-of-the-century gardens as part of an ongoing national Garden Club of America project. "The 1920s and late teens was the golden age of gardening and residential architecture in Cleveland," said White. "There were fabulous garden designs by prestigious landscape architects like Warren Manning and Frederick Law Olmsted. Unfortunately, there isn't much left of the gardens. But in the Stan Hywet Hall walled garden, you can see the restored garden designed by Ellen Shipman after Warren Manning's original design. Her design is so complex—she believed in loading a garden with perennials and potted flowers that would be replaced as they went out of flower. Her drawing is very specific and tightly tacked together—it's impossible for anyone but a well staffed organization like Stan Hywet Hall to duplicate."

To find out what has happened to the hundreds of other fabulous early twentieth-century gardens, White looks for old photos, post cards, and magazine illustrations. "Anyone could write about a garden in a book or journal but there isn't proof that it was actually done. A photo proves that at least somebody tried it," White explains. She has tracked down old garden and landscape photos in the Western Reserve Historical Society archives and at the Ohio Historical Society in Columbus. She now finds most new leads when she gives talks and audience members recall some old literature or correspondence stashed in their own attics.

When White finds an interesting garden that she wants to put in the Smithsonian collection, she must seek out pages full of information, including address, landscape architect, successive owners, types of plants, and present condition. She even traced one wrought-iron garden gate from Francis Drury's home to the Adult Parole Board of the Ohio Prison System.

"This project is like eating peanuts," says White. "We keep looking for more." If you have any historic garden photos in your attic, write to Connie White at P.O. Box 11, Gates Mills, 44040.

Further Reading

More information on these and other subjects related to historical horticulture can be found in back issues of *Western Reserve Magazine*. Many historical gardening volumes can be found in the rare book collection of The Garden Center of Greater Cleveland. Or consult the Dittrick Museum of Medical History at Case Western Reserve University, a rare book collection of herbals and catalogs housed in the Allen Memorial Library (11000 Euclid Avenue, Cleveland; 368-3648).

To learn more about the Shakers of northeast Ohio, see *In The Valley of God's Pleasure* (by Carolyn Piercy, 1951, Stratford House, NY) and various manuscripts preserved in the Shaker Historical Museum (16740 South Park Boulevard, Shaker Heights; 921-1201).

You can find out more about early landscapes in: *Treatise on the Theory and Practice of Landscape Gardening Adapted to North America* (by Andrew Jackson Downing, 1841 [original], 1991 [reprint], Dumbarton Oaks, Washington, D.C.) and *The Golden Age of Gardens* (by Mac Griswold and Eleanor Weller, 1991, Abrams Publishing, New York, NY).

And, if you're ever in Washington, D.C., check out the

Garden Club of America's historical slide collection on laser disk at the Smithsonian Institution.

CHAPTER SIX

～

Common Concerns
of Area Gardeners

ALONG WITH A SET OF basic natural resources, Cleveland area gardeners share many common concerns. Some general gardening questions are heard again and again all around town: How can I best deal with the clay in my soil? What can I do with a shady lot? What plantings will work best with my landscape? Is it necessary to spray my lawn to keep it perfect and green? Should I plant wildflowers to save a bit of our natural heritage?

If you have struggled with any of these issues, you are not alone. It is important to consider these and other major topics of general gardening interest that apply specifically to our Cleveland area gardens.

DEALING WITH CLAY

Working in clay is a problem for many Cleveland-area gardeners. In general, where clay is common, be careful to lighten the soil (make it fluffy so excess water can drain out and the roots will have access to air), and eliminate the excess water, or plants will perish. James Storer, district conservationist with the U.S. Department of Agriculture Soil Conservation Service, says, "People think that if you dig a hole and fill it with peat and sand it will be a good place to grow a plant. But that just doesn't work in this clay soil. When it rains, the water will fill up the hole like a bathtub and will only drain out as fast as the surrounding area—which is not fast at all."

An Expert Solution

One gardener who has success in clay soil is Tom Yates, garden superintendent at Holden Arboretum's Lantern Court, a former estate in Kirtland (see Gardens Open to the Public, chapter 1). Yates has found a solution agreeable to hundreds of species and varieties of flowers; rather than attempt to change clay, he exploits its ability to hold moisture and nutrients with a surprisingly simple procedure.

When he began working at Lantern Court in 1972, Yates imagined the estate as an idea garden and showplace. He proposed underplanting specimen trees with perennials and adding drifting beds of flowers, rock gardens, wildflower gardens, and ericaceous (heath-type) thickets. But Yates soon realized that the major problem facing these plans was the heavy yellow clay and wet clay topsoil. He struggled to amend the clay with sand, but it dried into hard brick. He tried to dig the soil especially deep and enrich it with black soil collected near a pond, but the resulting bed stayed swampy and wet.

Then it occurred to Yates to build a new bed over the once-promising black loam. He blanketed the prospective garden with two inches of silica sand and a six-inch layer of wood chips. He could then plant directly in the raised bed without further soil amendment. "The plants grow beautifully there now, and I seldom need to water," he said. The clay acts like a sponge of moisture and a reserve of nutrients that plant roots can reach while the well-drained organic layer on the top stays light and dry so roots and shoots won't rot.

Since that time, Yates has refined his soil blend. Most Lantern Court beds are composed of 40 percent finished compost, 20 percent leaf compost, 20 percent silica sand (which is not alkaline and will not influence the pH), and 20 percent year-old horse manure. This blend supports gardens of daffodils and daylilies, primroses and violets, wildflowers and hosta, barren strawberries, and hardy leadworts—all with equal success.

For acid-loving ericaceous plants (such as azaleas, heathers, bearberry, hudsonia, and cassiope) and for bog plants (such as pitcher plants, cardinal flowers, Japanese iris, and trollius), Yates makes a slightly different blend. He mixes sphagnum peat, oak-leaf compost, sand, and white pine needles and lays the mixture over a six-inch layer of silica sand.

For rare specialities that require an extra-acid soil (trailing arbutus, for example), Yates combines silica sand, pine needles, rotting pine and oak logs, bark, and wood chips. "Although this sounds bizarre, the rotting logs can make the difference between success and failure with trailing arbutus," Yates said.

All of these methods are intended to be easy to imitate in home gardens. "If we claim to need unfamiliar or expensive products, we are not serving the public," Yates said.

When Is a Soil Not a Soil?

Eighty percent of Tom Yates's planting mix is not really soil at all but organic matter. "We're greedy for organics," he said. "We chase after utility line crews to get wood chips, collect pine needles from the grove across the street, and use loads and loads of horse manure" (which he lets age for a year before use).

Yates takes all these panhandled materials, as well as seedless weeds, and composts them for about two years in rows that are 20 feet long, three feet high, and three feet wide.

Autumn leaves get a slightly different treatment: he puts them in square bins of snow fencing for a year, then moistens the decaying leaf pile and covers them with black plastic for a second year; after that they are ready to recycle into gardens. Both processes take a lot of time and space but require minimal labor and produce a reliable source of organic matter every year.

Clay at Claystone

"There was nothing on our property but a house when we bought it," said Don Vanderbrook, Cleveland-area floral designer and owner of Claystone, his home and four-acre formal garden. "There was a meadow on the hillside behind the house. I began putting in beds of cut flowers there but every time I rototilled, all the clay would slide down. So I terraced the hillside and raised all the beds with railroad ties. Clay soil is very heavy but wonderful when it's broken up. We have lots of horse manure—we keep three horses because they look so great out there, and they supply the fertilizer and compost we've been adding for years. Now the soil is fantastic. You can sink your hands into it and feel the beautiful texture."

USING LIME

If your soil is overly acidic, as is common around Cleveland, you may need to use lime. Lime is short for limestone, which can sweeten—or raise—a soil's pH value (the measure of soil acidity or alkalinity). You can use lime to change the kinds of nutrients that are available in the soil, curtail certain fungus diseases, and generally improve the performance of plants that prefer alkaline soils (such as baby's breath). But lime should never be applied indiscriminately, without knowing if you need it and how much you need, or the soil's chemistry may be thrown out of alignment.

Gardeners use lime to counteract acids that are left in soil by decaying leaves, mulches, and other organic matter. Acids also accumulate from applied fertilizers and from the weathering of minerals within the soil. If these acids build up to excessive levels and are not counteracted by soil sweeteners (such as calcium and magnesium), the soil can become too acidic to grow plants well.

First, Test
To find out if overly acidic soil is causing limited success in your yard, get your soil's pH value tested. (The pH value is judged on a scale of 1 to 14: 7 is neutral, below 7 is acid, and above 7 is alkaline.) You can buy inexpensive pH test kits or have soil samples checked by the County Cooperative Extension Service (Cuyahoga: 631-1890, Geauga: 834-4656, Lake: 357-2582, Lorain: 322-0127, Medina: 725-4911, Summit: 497-1611).

If your soil's pH value is:

• Near pH 6.5, the optimum pH for most plants, your soil is slightly acidic, but don't bother to add lime unless you have perennial baby's breath or plants native to alkaline soils.
• Lower than pH 6, your soil is slightly too acidic for most plants, and you may need to add some lime. Exceptions are acid-loving ericacious rhododendrons, azaleas, mountain laurels, Japanese andromeda (*Pieris japonica*), and leucothoe, which need an acidic soil.
• Neutral pH 7 or even a slightly alkaline pH 7.5, your soil is adequate for many plants except those acid-lovers just mentioned.
• Higher than pH 8, your soil is too alkaline for most

plants. This may mean someone added too much lime in the past. You might need to counteract the excess lime by adding sulfur.

Adjusting pH

Whenever you manipulate soil pH, follow the recommendations that come with the soil test results or on the lime-bag label. And choose the kind of lime you use with care.

Calcitic limestone contains calcium carbonate, which is simply ground up limestone—inexpensive and effective. Dolomitic limestone is magnesium carbonate, an alkaline material and source of the nutrient magnesium. Both of these are available in different-sized particles. Finer grinds will break down in soil more quickly; coarser grinds are released more slowly. A mixture of fine and coarse grades is good in most cases because it can both correct a pH problem promptly and keep acids neutralized for some time thereafter. Another product you'll see is quicklime, calcium oxide. When you add water to this it becomes hydrated lime, which works fast—fast enough to burn plant roots if you use too much. It also can produce a gas that kills turf if applied at the same time as fertilizer containing ammonia.

Making and Using Compost

What Is Compost?

Organic matter (decayed plant and animal debris) lightens heavy soils. It also helps make sandy soils moister, releases a wide variety of nutrients gently, and encourages abundant underground life (earthworms, beneficial bacteria, and fungi) that help splants grow better.

A fine source of organic matter is compost: properly recycled garden waste and landscape debris. As a soil conditioner, compost can be as good as commercial products sold in garden centers.

Because landscape debris is no longer welcome in most landfills, many communities turn leaves and grass clippings into garden compost, which they then sell or provide free to residents. The independent and nonprofit Greater Cleveland Ecology Program (687-1266) collects landscape and garden waste from several communities and markets Cuyahoga Leaf Humus, which can even be ordered for home delivery. The city of Solon (248-1155) gives finished humus away free to residents who pick it up in their own bags or buckets. Westlake (871-3300) and Bay Village (871-2200) work jointly; they sell and deliver their finished compost within city limits.

Making and Using Your Own Compost

It's not too hard to make your own compost using old vegetation from around your yard. When you have a ready supply, you can:

• Work compost into new beds. Start with a two-inch layer of compost in an eight-inch-deep bed.

• Use compost to mulch existing plantings. The nutrients will trickle down to plant roots with the rain, and the compost will work down to condition the soil when you weed or hoe.

• Put a bucketful into a planting hole and work it into surrounding soil to help a new plant get off to a good start.

When you make your own compost, you can choose from easy but slow-acting compost processes or more time-consuming but quicker-acting methods. The composting process itself is really not much different from gardening. But instead of encouraging plants to grow, you are encouraging them to decay. Create a flora of decomposers (bacteria and fungi) that live in soil and tear apart fallen tissues. They work best when given warmth, moisture, oxygen, and a little nitrogen—all of which you can provide as you build your compost pile.

If you blend the right kinds of plant debris and turn or fluff the pile regularly, decomposers will work most quickly, creating a "hot" compost pile. If you are more casual about the pile, it will still decompose, only slowly and without building up much heat; hence the name "cool" composting.

Hot Composting

The simplest way to start hot composting is by blending a hot pile, which you can leave out in the open or enclose in a frame of wire mesh or snow fencing. Begin by gathering enough plant scraps to build a pile three feet wide and four feet high and deep. To get this much debris takes some planning. Perhaps some Saturday you can renovate a flower or vegetable garden, do a little pruning, rake the leaves, and mow the lawn. On Sunday, assemble the remains of your efforts into a compost pile.

Separate soft greenery, such as lawn clippings and weeds (which provide nitrogen as they decay), from harder dry vegetation, such as straw, twigs, or dried leaves. If you have a lot of really hard material like wood chips, add extra nitrogen fertilizer. Chop clippings and leaves with a lawn mower and soft woody material with a garden shredder if you want them to decompose faster.

Then pile the two components in alternating layers of two inches of green matter and four inches of brown. Sprinkle good organic soil, finished compost, or store-bought inoculant (decay microorganisms in granular form) in between each layer to provide the decomposers.

Keep the pile moist, but not wet. Let plenty of air percolate inside by turning the pile upside down or fluffing it with a garden fork at least once a month. The compost will be finished when it turns into a crumbly brown mound and you can no longer identify the original components.

For those interested in speeding up the process (at a price), there are also several commercial composting systems available. These include spinning barrels or specially ventilated plastic bins that accelerate the heating process and produce compost fast.

Cool Composting

To cool compost, simply add plant debris to a pile as you gather it; then wait for nature to slowly turn it into organic matter. Because decomposition can take a couple years, you should make a new pile every year or else you will simply bury what has decomposed under new debris.

Another easy way to cool compost is to grind up your old plant scraps with a lawn mower or shredder and layer them on top of a garden bed. In a couple of months, they seem to disappear and return to the soil.

What About Animal Manure?

Having both horse and garden makes a lot of sense. But not everyone can, or wants, to keep a four-footed manure machine around. Luckily, there is an excess in this area (including nearby Geauga County, which has a larger horse population than any other county in Ohio). You can get horse manure free at many stables, especially because stable owners are now required by federal and state legislation to meet more exacting manure-handling laws. The changes are coming about because manure, as a recyclable material, is being restricted from landfills. Furthermore, if manure piles up in areas where rainwater can carry nutrients and bacteria into streams and ground water, it is now considered a pollutant.

"It's easy for nutrients to get away if there is any slope to the land at all," said Al Bonnis, agent for the Ohio Soil and Water Conservation District. "Then you are washing nutrients down the drain. We want to see the manure spread on farm fields or pastures where it can do some good, or given to someone who can use it for gardening or compost."

Manure contains a complex blend of nutrients—it's an ideal slow-release fertilizer. The manure produced by one horse in 37 days is enough to produce a bushel of corn. In this area, however, horse manure usually comes mixed with the wood shavings used for bedding, which breaks down very slowly and absorbs nitrogen as it goes. You can avoid the problems associated with wood bedding if you can locate aged manure or a stable that beds their horses in straw. You can also mix thin layers of manure and wood bedding into a compost pile; add a little extra nitrogen (a sprinkling of lawn fertilizer, for example) if there is more wood shavings than manure.

Composting horse manure solves the other problem associated with horse waste: weeds. By letting the manure heat up and decay, you kill many of the weed seeds that horses eat and pass intact. If you use horse manure in a relatively fresh form, be prepared to do plenty of weeding for the next growing season.

Gardening Despite Shade

Many of the older parts of Cleveland and the surrounding suburbs have wonderful mature shade trees that provide a cool escape from the burning heat of summer.

But this shade, though soft and cooling, also poses problems for gardeners. The deeper the shade, the fewer kinds of plants you can grow in it. So scan carefully the varying intensities of shade in your yard to get a good idea of what you are dealing with.

The earth on the north side of a building and beneath an evergreen tree remains deeply shaded throughout the year, but light penetrates below a deciduous tree. The amount depends on the fullness and height of its canopy. To achieve light shade, fine-textured trees such as honey and black locust (which do suffer from pest problems in northeast Ohio), birch, and Japanese pagoda (*Sophora japonica*) fill the bill. Don't forget such well-adapted Cleveland trees as oak, hickory, ash, linden, Chinese elm, sour gum, tulip tree, and willow. When you thin their branches or remove the lower ones to a height of 30 to 50 feet, you create extra light and increased air circulation. You may be able to grow shade-tolerant lawn grasses in this case. Or you could plant a bed of shade-tolerant ornamentals, including small trees, shrubs, and flowers.

Planning for Shade

Use a shade garden near the street to muffle traffic noise or to screen out an unpleasant view; use it on the south or west side of your home to cool it in summer. Grow a shade garden near the patio to provide scenery when you relax outdoors in summer. If you have a wooded area, fit it with a winding path, some stones, fallen logs, and other natural sculpture and encourage wildflowers and ferns to brighten it up. These schemes, however, will only work if you give your shade garden some thought before planting so that it will grow well right from the start.

Use shade-tolerant or shade-loving plants (see the following section). When you buy nursery stock to use in a shady area, always check with the nursery to see if the shrub has been raised in full sun or shade. If grown in full sun and transplanted to shade, even the most versatile shrub may drop leaves and branches haphazardly. If you are planting in the woods, look for ground covers that will not escape and take over wild areas. Stay away from periwinkle and ivy (which are abundant in the Metroparks and other local woods); instead try ferns, *Epimediums*, European ginger, and bugleweed. Where shade is too heavy for growing most plants well, use a neat, simple mulch of bark or pebbles instead of plantings.

In addition to the challenges of shade, root competition can be severe under trees. Because our soil tends to be heavy, most trees root primarily in the top 12 to 18 inches of soil, the same root zone as flowers, shrubs, and lawn. Silver maples, sugar maples, and beech trees—common in local landscapes—are especially shallow-rooted and seldom leave any rooting space for other species. It's best to plant outside the canopy of mature trees, where their roots generally end and where rainwater will fall freely, unimpeded by the tree canopy.

If you need to plant beneath a tree, you can remove roots in small areas that you intend to plant. Or spread up to six inches of good topsoil over the tree roots where you intend to plant—no deeper or wider or you could damage the tree. Plant promptly so the new specimens can get established before the tree roots also spread into the new soil. Then water and fertilize regularly, especially during droughts, to keep these plants from competing for moisture and nutrients.

Good Species for Northeast Ohio Shade Gardens

When planting a shade garden, choose ornamental plants that are well adapted to our climate and that will be interesting in spring, summer, fall—even winter. Here are some possibilities:

Spring
- Chinese witch hazel (a small tree with spidery yellow flowers)
- Cornelian dogwood (a large shrub with small yellow flowers; the first of the dogwood clan to bloom in spring)
- Spicebush (a native bush with early-blooming greenish-yellow flowers and scented twigs and leaves that is quite tolerant of difficult shady situations)
- Shadblow (*Amelanchier* species; trees with willowy white blossoms and attractive bark)
- Spring bulbs that grow before trees leaf out, including daffodils, squill, wood hyacinth, snowdrops, winter aconite

Summer
- Blueberries (eat the berries and enjoy the handsome fall foliage)
- Rhododendrons and azaleas (later blooming types)
- Summer-sweet (*Clethra alnifolia*) (a bush that bears small fragrant flowers and is tolerant of sun or shade)
- Perennials such as bleeding heart, coralbells, astilbe, columbine, cardinal flower, blue lobelia, and hosta

Fall
- Shrubs with bold autumn leaf color, such as viburnums, winged euonymus, and blueberries
- Witch hazel (the flowers appear as leaves are falling)
- Perennials such as Japanese anemones

Nontoxic Alternatives for Lawn Care

Spring has traditionally been the time to douse a lawn with chemicals so that it will grow like green velvet. Recently, however, Cleveland-area communities have been questioning the wisdom of following a regular schedule of pesticide, herbicide, and fertilizer treatments. Many of the synthetic products used on lawns simply are not necessary. They cost a bundle of money, whether you do the application yourself or hire someone else to do it, and the salts and chemicals they leave behind can leach into rivers, lakes, and ground water.

Aerate and Fertilize

Mark Druckenbrod, horticulturist and assistant director at The Garden Center of Greater Cleveland, says good nontoxic alternatives for improving lawn growth include aeration and organic fertilizers: "Because we have heavy clay that we compact every time we walk across the lawn, aerating the soil in spring will do wonders." Aeration in late summer or fall is recommended by Richard Kay of Breezewood Gardens; he says it encourages root growth, making grasses healthier the following spring.

To aerate, hire a landscaper or rent a heavy-duty lawn-mower-type aerator that cuts cores—small cylinders—out of the lawn. The openings they leave behind let air and moisture penetrate down through the thatch and clay to the turf roots. The unearthed plugs break up on top of surface thatch (the matted remains of old grass tillings), speeding its decomposition. Request the kind of aerator that has hollow tubes or cylinders set on a rotating drum. Brands that sport large spikes simply dent the soil and make the compression worse.

"Aerating regularly," according to Druckenbrod, "lets grass plants grow a deeper and better root system. And if you do it every spring for a number of years you'll end up covering about every part of the lawn. Then it is all rejuvenated."

With fertilizers, many lawn experts are finding less can be better. "People need to lower their standards," Druckenbrod said. "There is no need for picture-perfect show-quality lawns. That kind of perfection takes overkill in time, money, and chemicals." When you fertilize three times during spring and summer (an old recommendation), the lawn stays constantly growing and needs a lot of water to stay healthy. This is an extravagant system from an environmental and economic point of view, and also timewise, because the lawn needs constant mowing.

Lawns that contain bluegrass, as do most of ours, need one fertilization. If you use a standard lawn fertilizer, apply half of a one-time dose in April (or September) and the second half a month or two later. Or use organic or slow-release fertilizers that provide their nutrients over the entire summer. With them, one application is plenty.

If insect or weed problems arise, don't just blanket the yard with a pesticide or herbicide. Take some time to identify the problem and to seek out the least toxic method for dealing with it. Spot-treat, if possible, attacking only the source of the problem and not surrounding areas. If you have a few weeds, pull them out. If you have beetle grubs eating turf roots, treat the lawn with a grubicide in combination with milky spore bacteria, which will help prevent Japanese beetle grubs.

For more information on lawn care, see *Building a Healthy Lawn: A Safe and Natural Approach* (by Stewart Franklin, 1988, Garden Way Publishing, Pownal, VT).

A Victorian Lawn Is an Easy Alternative

There is a special appeal to uniformity in a lawn of grass and nothing but grass, but there is also virtue in a modest amount of diversity. If we all looked alike, life would be boring indeed. The same is true of lawns, although this opinion may represent a minority in these parts. But consider your other options before spraying, treating, mowing, watering, raking, and thatching your way to a model green turf.

Good grass is hard to achieve. It falls victim to too little water, too much water (both common around here), and pests and diseases that easily spread from lawn to lawn. And when you get that wonderful grass growing healthily, what does it mean? Mowing, and lots of it.

Consider instead the Victorian lawn, beloved early in this century when chemicals were not so abundant and when mowing was powered by hand and back. The Victorian lawn in this region had pretty small flowers like forget-me-nots, veronica, violets, creeping phlox, and other desirables that made it interesting. They crept into the grass on their own and grew where they were well adapted. That meant the homeowner didn't have to do anything to ensure their survival and they took much less work.

In today's lawn, homeowners often are upset by white clover that spreads amid the turf. To get rid of it, you can apply herbicides, reseed, water intensively, and hope to encourage new grass growing thickly enough to discourage the colonization of other plants. On the other hand, clover stays green all summer, despite the worst heat and drought. Its flowers are attractive even though they are different from the ordinary green lawn, and because they are legumes they actually can add nitrogen to the soil, fertilizing nearby grasses naturally. Not a bad combination.

This is not to say that you should let dandelions, sedges, and other unattractive weeds spread through the lawn. You will still have to spot-treat those undesirables. But at the same time, you can be a little more tolerant of the handsome wild species while minimizing the amount of chemicals you use.

Home Landscaping:
FOUNDATION PLANTINGS

Bad landscape design isn't pretty: windows look out into the backs of shrubs, large tree limbs dangle perilously over the roof, and the overall view is awkward, contrived, or overgrown. Such a landscape only gets worse with time. If you're dissatisfied with your landscape, or if you are moving to a new home, it's time to take a fresh look at the plants surrounding your walls.

Some of the most common problems that occur in our landscapes involve poorly designed foundation plantings. Foundation plantings have evolved and expanded over the decades, reflecting changes in home architecture, available plants, and gardening styles. However, some old-fashioned, or even obsolete, concepts still persist in this area; they can stifle a landscape.

Foundation plantings, always in the public eye, can be a way for you to beautify and increase the value of your home and to exercise your creativity. If you invest some time in planning, you can create an attractive design in which maintenance is minimized and plants will flourish for years.

The Purpose of Foundation Planting
The idea of enveloping the face of a house with trees and shrubs originated when basements were shallow and cement walls protruded above the ground to allow space for coal-powered furnaces. To hide the unattractive mechanics of con-

struction, gardeners trooped in shrubbery soldiers and lined them up as a visual barricade.

Modern homes seldom reveal tall expanses of cement foundations, lessening the need for concealment. Still, the home landscape will benefit from carefully designed plantings that soften harsh architectural lines and unite the home with the surrounding property.

Just as homes have changed, plants suitable for foundation plantings are more numerous and better refined. Homeowners are no longer limited to the old landscaping standbys of the historic Western Reserve, such as privet and lilac—both of which mature tall enough to obscure most first-floor windows. Today you can find a wealth of dwarf plants that fit around a foundation without overgrowing (though you may have to seek them out if you buy locally).

Foundation plantings can be simple and understated or elaborate. The simplest option is the traditional line of woody plants in front of a house. More modern alternatives feature beds of arcing lines that may drift out into the foreground of the yard. Either style will be attractive if you pay attention to some fundamental rules of design. How you select and arrange plants should echo interesting house features, soften angles, and draw attention to a focal point—usually the front door.

Start With the House

Begin by thinking about lines. Houses are heavy in vertical lines, which are strongest at the outer corners of the house and the doorway. Neutralize their stiffness with the horizontal branching of rounded shrubs and small trees. The tallest plants, usually located at the corners of the house, should not exceed two-thirds of the height of the roof line. The entryway also can call for tall accent plants, but these should remain lower than eave level. Or you can substitute lower-growing plants instead that draw the eye with color, form, or texture. Fill in between the entryway and house corners with compact shrubs to create a concave or downsloping line that lets the eye pass easily to the doorway.

How high plants should go depends on your house. For a small one-story house, stick with low plants. For a large Victorian house, you can use taller shrubs but avoid blocking doors and windows. A split-level home may call for a small flowering tree at the single-story end and a shrub hedge at the two-story side to balance the shape of the house.

In most cases, the simplest plan is the best. If you limit yourself, for instance, to three different kinds of plants, you can cluster and repeat to give a subtle rhythm to the plan. It's a good idea to mix deciduous with evergreen. The ever-changing deciduous plants progress from flowers to fruits to fall color, while evergreens stand steadfast year-round.

Try to match the plants' ambience to your house. Color is always important, but so is the texture created by leaf size, branching pattern, and bark. For a home of wood siding, a shrub of medium texture will not obtrude. Brick or barn siding is complemented by larger leaves, such as oakleaf hydrangea.

The shape of the planting bed adds to the overall effect. Lines can reflect the shape of the building. Large curves, carefully planned, can further soften architectural angles. However, free-form beds may look contrived and alien. To make them natural, curve and reverse the curve, with large sweeping lines, not little wiggles.

Plant Size
You may decide to let the foundation planting drift out into an entry garden suitable for low shrubs, perennials, or annual

flowers. A small specimen tree could be balanced by a cluster of shrubs on the opposite side of the entrance.

Before you run out and buy a single plant, learn the mature height and spread of each shrub and tree you intend to include in your design. Calculate their spacing to let them assume their full size without squeezing their neighbors into odd, one-sided shapes.

A little research into the mature sizes of trees will prevent future problems from limbs that bump into the house or snag utility lines. The height to which some trees can soar may be hard to imagine when you see young nursery stock in a pot: a 5-foot red maple tree can grow to 120 feet in our region; a Christmas-tree-sized white pine can reach 80 feet. Trees of this size should be planted well away from the house. Up close, it is safer to stick with smaller trees, such as the paper-bark maple, which reaches 25 to 30 feet, or the fringe tree, which grows 12 to 25 feet tall—both especially good species for this area.

There are giants among shrubs as well. Forsythia, common in landscapes around town, will reach 10 feet—well above most windowsills. Thinning these shrubs annually will keep them in check. So many nice dwarf shrubs are available, how-ever, that it doesn't make sense to bother with an oversized plant. Try viburnums, barberries, false cypress, rhododen-drons, spruces, hollies, junipers, and yews; all need little or no care after planting and are available in the Cleveland area (though you may have to order early).

Avoiding Trouble

Once you have identified the right plants for your house, be sure they will receive the sun and rain necessary for good growth. A roof overhang is like an umbrella that keeps the soil below dry and barren. Situate all plants at least one foot away from the roof's outer edge. This safety zone also saves the day when the gutters dam up and drench the soil below with rain, or when heavy wet snow plummets off the roof. Likewise, if you will be planting near a walkway, add from 6 to 12 inches to allow for the mature spread of a plant. This way, branches can droop when wet or snow-laden without invading the walk.

Plants, of course, need sunlight, but houses can be particularly baffling because they will intensify as well as block sunlight. If the foundation planting will be on the north side, shadow may cover much of the bed most of the day. It will stay dark and damp, limiting your plant choices. Light-colored houses will reflect sun, especially on the southern side, and can burn even a hardy sun-lover. Check the number of hours the sun shines in each location, then buy a plant suited to that light exposure. If you try to keep a shade plant in bright sun or vice versa, chances are good that you will be disappointed.

You must reckon with difficulties dealt by pavement and underground utilities as well. Know where underground wires and pipes are located. Avoid disturbing them when landscaping, and keep deep-rooted plants some distance away. Likewise, you may need to give extra space to plantings near driveways and walks; these surfaces radiate heat and limit rooting space and water penetration.

Soil is also a concern. The natural topsoil on your home site may have been removed or compacted during construction. Infertile subsurface soil unearthed when digging the basement may end up on top. This can leave soil heavy and wet, possibly requiring the addition of drainage tiles before plants will grow well.

Plant Selection

The following lists include some of the species that thrive in northeast Ohio and are seldom bothered by pests and diseases. Unfortunately, it excludes some of the most common landscape plants, such as our native flowering dogwood, blue spruce, and European white birch. Although they are handsome plants, they are plagued by pests and diseases and not easy to keep healthy. Boxwood is not included here either, although people continue to try to grow it; most cultivars are not hardy enough to last more than several years. Rhododendrons and azaleas also can be difficult where the soil is heavy clay—so build them a bed of well-drained soil that is rich in organic matter or don't bother to deal with them at all.

(For more information on selecting plants, see *Manual of Woody Landscape Plants*, by Michael Dirr, 1988, Stipes Publishing, Champaign, IL.)

Special Small Trees
• Paperbark maple (*Acer griseum*) has handsome peeling bark and reaches 20 to 30 feet tall
• Japanese maple (*Acer palmatum*) is available in standard, cut-leaf and red-leaf forms from 6 to 25 feet high
• Allegheny serviceberry (*Amelanchier laevis*) reaches about 25 feet, bearing white flowers in spring and berries that birds love in summer
• White fringetree (*Chionanthus virginicus*) can grow to 20 feet tall with 8-inch-long, fragrant plumes of white flowers in late spring
• Kousa dogwood (*Cornus kousa*) stretches up to about 20 feet tall and wide, bearing white flowers in June
• Common witch hazel (*Hamamelis virginiana*) grows up to 30 feet high and 25 feet wide, and bears spidery yellow flowers when the leaves fall in autumn
• Crab apples (*Malus* species) can be wonderful small trees, with handsome flowers and fruit, if you use disease-resistant (or at least disease-tolerant) and compact-sized cultivars.

Some to look for include *Malus floribunda*, 'Indian Summer', or 'Sugar Tyme', or cultivars from the extra-dwarf Round Table series, including 'Camelot', 'Excalibur', and 'Hamlet'
- Japanese tree lilac (*Syringa reticulata*) grows up to 30 feet tall and 25 feet wide, bearing fragrant, 10-inch-long panicles of white flowers in June

Suitably Small Shrubs
You can keep small shrubs even smaller than their mature height with minimal pruning (See Proper Pruning, in March entry, chapter 7)
- Korean barberry (*Berberis koreana*) matures into a 4 to 6 feet tall, rounded and thorny shrub
- Japanese barberry (*Berberis thunbergii*) stays as low as 3 feet tall, and some cultivars have bright yellow or maroon foliage
- Japanese beautyberry (*Callicarpa japonica*) can reach 6 feet tall and wide, and bears pink or white flowers in summer and purple berries in fall
- False cypress (*Chamaecyparis* species) stays smaller if you choose dwarf cultivars, which have interesting evergreen foliage
- Sweet pepper bush (*Clethra alnifolia*) reaches up to 8 feet high and 6 feet wide with small fragrant white or pink flowers in summer. It's one of the few that bloom in August.
- Cotoneasters (*Cotoneaster apiculatus* and *horizontalis*) stay under 3 feet high but spread up to 6 or 8 feet wide. They have small pink or white flowers in spring, red berries in fall and small glossy leaves
- Smooth hydrangea (*Hydrangea arborescens*) and oakleaf hydrangea (*Hydrangea quercifolia*) can reach 5 feet tall and wide, bearing flat clusters of white flowers in summer
- Japanese holly (*Ilex crenata*) includes dwarf forms that

stay 4 to 5 feet tall—some even lower—with small glossy-green leaves similar to boxwood
- Northern bayberry (*Myrica pensylvanica*) reaches 5 to 9 feet tall and carries waxy, gray, bayberry-scented berries in winter
- Yews (*Taxus* species) are available in dwarf cultivars such as *T. baccata* 'Nana' (3 feet high) and 'Chadwickii' (reaches about 4 feet high; named after an Ohio State University horticulture professor)
- Koreanspice viburnum (*Viburnum carlesii*) can grow from 5 to 8 feet tall, bearing fragrant white flowers in spring and handsome fall color
- *Viburnum plicatum* 'Newzam', stays 30 inches high and bears white flowers

Plants for Screening Out Unattractive Views
- Bottlebrush buckeye (*Aesculus parviflora*) spreads to 12 feet high and 15 feet wide and bears 12-inch-long panicles of white flowers in midsummer
- Winged euonymus (*Euonymus alata*) reaches 20 feet high—the 'Compacta' form stays smaller—with wonderful bright fall color and interesting stems in winter
- Rugosa rose (*Rosa rugosa*), a prickly stemmed summer-flowering rose that will grow up to 10 feet high and 15 feet wide; it does not suffer as much from diseases that trouble other roses

Long-Blooming Perennials
These perennials naturally put on an extended show and will bloom even longer if you cut off the old flowers:

- Blanket flower (*Gaillardia* x *grandiflora*)
- Catmint (*Nepeta faassenii*)

- Coneflower (*Rudbeckia fulgida*) 'Goldsturm'
- Daisy fleabane (*Erigeron* 'Profusion')
- Daylily (*Hemerocallis*) 'Happy Returns' and 'Stella d'Oro'
- *Hibiscus* 'Disco Belle'
- Purple coneflower (*Echinacea purpurea*)
- Russian sage (*Perovskia atriplicifolia*)
- *Salvia* species
- *Scabiosa caucasica*
- Speedwell (*Veronica*) 'Sunny Border Blue'
- Stokes' aster (*Stokesia laevis*)
- Tickseed (*Coreopsis*, *C. verticillata* 'Moonbeam', 'Zagreb', 'Golden Showers' and *C. lanceolata* 'Early Sunrise', 'Sunray' and *C. rosea*).

For more information, see Northern Ohio Perennial Society entry in Plant Societies, chapter 4 or *Perennials for American Gardens* (by Ruth Rogers Clausen and Nicolas Ekstrom, 1989, Random House, New York, NY).

PROPER PLANTING

Newly planted trees and shrubs are dying all over greater Cleveland wherever the soils are heavy. Many of these plants are smothering because whoever transplanted them didn't know where the roots were. Fred Robinson, consulting arborist, has been called to the scene of many dying plants and has dug up enough failing trees and shrubs to identify several fatal mistakes transplanters make. Primarily, they overlook the fact that some balled and burlapped plants have deep root collars (the place where the stem emerges from the root system) and thus even deeper roots.

"I have found the root collar to be 6 to 12 inches below the top of the ball in almost all cases of failure," Robinson said. "With the root collar so deep, the root system is limited to the bottom half of the ball."

Where soil is heavy, wet, or compacted, most plantsmen will plant balled and burlapped plants shallowly to keep the roots from drowning. This will hurt plants with deep root crowns. The top half of the ball, which is mostly soil, is left above ground while the bottom half, which contains all the roots, is trapped in a shallow hole. Water fills the hole, driving out oxygen; the plant soons suffocates, or drowns.

How does this occur? Robinson has traced part of the problem back to nurseries that grow material in loose sandy soils. These nurseries tend to plant field material deep for extra stability. The nurseries may also try to protect the roots by covering them more heavily than is ideal. In addition, workers might cultivate between rows, building up even more soil over the roots.

When digging plants, workers may measure the depth of the ball by starting at the top of the soil rather than the root collar. (The size of the ball is predetermined as the size needed to sustain that particular plant.) When they dig the ball of a plant with a deep root collar, they can sever a majority of the roots that would otherwise be in the ball. For instance, if the root collar is six inches deep, the bottom of the ball will not include six inches of essential roots left deeper in the soil. The dug ball does not coincide with the essential root system.

To avoid this problem, before buying any balled and burlapped trees or shrubs check to see where the root collar is. Sway the trunk back and forth slowly and note where the trunk pivots. If it pivots right at the top of the ball, then there are roots all the way to the top. But if you can move the trunk around in the ball, the roots start somewhere lower than the top of the ball. For shrubs and multistemmed trees, you could identify the location of the root collar by probing down the trunk or cutting through the burlap near the stems, working carefully to avoid scarring the plant or weakening the ball.

Once you've located the root collar, measure the root system's depth. Armed with this knowledge, you can dig your holes accordingly.

One Expert's Technique

Richard Kay of Breezewood Gardens recommends the following planting technique, which his landscape crews use quite successfully:

1. Build an elevated planting bed by covering the existing soil with six inches of topsoil and one to two inches of peat moss, leaf humus, compost, or other kinds of organic matter. Mix the soil blend together with a rototiller.

2. Dig a hole deep enough for three-quarters of the root ball. The top one-quarter of the root ball should remain above the surface of the soil.

3. Make the hole as wide as possible, at least one foot wider than the diameter of the roots. This will allow roots to grow and spread easily.

4. Amend the soil you will put back into the planting hole. Add thirty to fifty percent organic matter. You can also add a water-holding polymer (a product that looks like crystals in the package but swells to resemble gelatin when moist) that helps plants survive heavy rain by absorbing excess water. The polymer also helps plants tolerate drought by releasing moisture reserves when the surrounding soil has dried out. After amending the backfill, use it to fill the hole in around the root ball.

5. Cover the top one-quarter of the root ball with two to three inches of mulch.

Finally, oxygen is as important for plant roots as moisture. Do not install sod or plant grass seed over the root system of a newly installed tree or shrub.

USING WILDFLOWERS CONSCIENTIOUSLY

Wildflowers, common along Ohio roadways and in unused fields and vacant Cleveland lots, are on the move, aided by natural and unnatural forces. Birds carry fleshy berries. Water tosses buoyant seed downstream. Winds lift lightweights with vegetable wings or plumes. In addition, people, trucks, and airplanes are moving more than their share. Thanks to modern communication and transportation systems, you can bring wildflowers from anywhere in the world to your doorstep. And Cleveland-area gardeners are doing so in ever-increasing numbers.

We no longer need to go out and cull seed or cuttings by hand. Instead, many gardeners will call one of the catalogs featuring color photos of thousands of Texas bluebonnets and California poppies all in riotous bloom. The UPS truck will deliver their blue mix or northern mix or can-of-color mix, which, it is hoped, will turn out like the catalog picture.

This scenario poses many exciting possibilities. But if you import wildflowers from far away, your wildflower garden is likely to prove disappointing. You may wish you had stuck with older methods and hand selected the best of the local wildflowers that are naturally fine-tuned to our climate and soil.

Among those who have been disappointed is the state of Ohio. When our state government decided to plant wildflowers along the highways in 1984, the job fell to the Ohio Department of Transportation (ODOT). Their staff soon discovered that there was no bulk source of Ohio seed for sale. So the Department of Transportation opted to buy seed mixes from a nursery in Colorado. They ended up with about thirty species of annuals, perennials, and biennials, many of which would never occur naturally in Ohio. One of the mixes included cultivars of baby's breath, purple and yellow coneflower, and bachelor's buttons; these were garden varieties and not wildflowers at all. Most of the mixes included European dame's rocket. With the exception of dame's rocket, none of these became self-proliferating.

"These plants grew fast and were showy. The gardens were so successful that people were pulling off the road to pick flowers or take photographs. However, soon they were overwhelmed by our natives and weeds. We found we had to replant annually," said Guy Denne, assistant chief of the Ohio Division of Natural Areas and Preserves. "We also found if we used dame's rocket by a waterway, it could escape into the surrounding countryside." It now blooms in abandon each May along Cleveland-area flood plains.

Select Carefully

These two problems—mixes of species doomed to failure or of those so aggressive they spread like a curse—occur again and again in mass plantings and intimate home wildflower meadows. But both can be avoided with careful species selection. One must assume the ODOT evaluated the mixes before they began the project, although their decision to plant non-natives has received criticism since then. Yet many home gardeners, including some of my own friends, admit to buying wildflower seed mixes blindly. They never stop to question what they are doing. They see the picture of the finished garden, read the promises, and are sold on the idea. If only people would approach purchasing wildflowers like grocery shopping. Would you buy a can of synthetic meat product if you didn't know what it was made of? Probably not. Likewise, how can you plant species if you don't know what they are?

Instead of jumping into wildflower gardening with your eyes closed, look closely at the fine print of the catalog or label before you buy a meadow mix. In many cases, you have to dig beneath the graphics and punchy language. Are the species identified somewhere? Is the product sanctioned by a reputable conservation association or native plant society? This is something the Eastern Native Plant Alliance hopes to begin soon. What percentage of the mix is short-lived annual seed, and what is longer lived perennial seed? Where does the seed come from? You probably won't find all the answers, but they are good questions to ask before you buy.

If there is no significant information on the package label, which does happen despite U.S. Department of Agriculture and state seed-labeling laws, look for a customer service phone number to get your answers. In most cases, you will find the wildflower mix you had your eye on is not local. Seed in it may come from out of state, region, or even country. With a little research, you might determine there are no species even remotely similar to those that grow in our neighborhoods.

Importing Trouble

Importing non-local wildflowers tends to disturb conservationists rather than to please them. "I have been among the people that complained to the Ohio Department of Transportation," said Allison Cusick, chief botanist for the Ohio Department of Natural Resources. "They shouldn't be using any European species, but the European stuff is cheaper than American natives."

Most naturalists and botanists agree that what you do in the privacy of your cultivated gardens is your own business. But what you do near wild areas affects everyone. European species such as dame's rocket can escape and spread into wild areas. This lanky white-to-purple flowering early summer bloomer is "a real weed," according to Jim Bissell, curator of botany for the Cleveland Museum of Natural History. "It seems we still have the same diversity of native species in those areas but the numbers of each species is way down," said Bissell.

Other aggressive alien species are worse than dame's rocket. You might compare the effect of these runaway aliens to foreign insect pests, such as gypsy moth, elm bark beetles, and Japanese beetles.

Perhaps the worst introduction in this area is purple loosestrife (*Lythrum salicaria* and *L. virgatum*), which have been sold as cultivated garden plants and wildflowers. These showy lavender-spiked wildflowers seed so prolifically that they have taken over thousands of acres of Ohio wetlands from native species. Even self-sterile garden cultivars of purple loosestrife can hybridize with the native species, *L. alatum*, and reproduce prolifically once again. Purple loosestrife has been a big problem in the wetlands along Lake Erie, but now the weed has spread along highway drainage ditches and the Ohio River. "I consider it one of the ten worst weeds in the state," said Cusick.

Dr. John Averett, botanist and director of research for the National Wildflower Research Center, explained the consequences of this kind of escaped alien. "Species like purple loosestrife take over and take up space that would have housed native plants. You alter the ecosystem by replacing a unique local plant with a species already present in another part of the world. The species tally comes up short in the end: the list of extinctions grows. And, since plants are at the bottom of the food chain, the effect reverberates up the ladder. Scientists estimate fourteen species of animals depend on each plant species. For each plant species lost to extinction, some wildlife will perish also," said Averett.

In Ohio, according to Cusick, purple loosestrife is threatening many of the common wetland plants, including broadleaved cattail and pickerel weed, and pushing endangered species such as white flowered wapato (*Sagittaria cuneata*) closer to extinction.

Loosestrife and dame's rocket are only two of the newest runaway aliens. Many of America's most common roadside wildflowers are actually European weeds or garden plants that have escaped and spread nearly nationwide. These include Queen Anne's lace, yarrow, chicory, and oxeye daisy. These four coexist with, or replace, other opportunistic native species in disturbed soils and along roadways. They are not the threat that purple loosestrife and, to a lesser extent, dame's rocket are because they seldom mass in more pristine sites where you would find rare and endangered plants.

Queen Anne's lace and its like are called naturalized exotics or aliens because they clearly came to America with the European colonization of the last five hundred years and thus are not native. But they have been on the continent over two hundred years, long enough for the more liberal nurserymen and gardeners to give them native status. You can find naturalized aliens included in many wildflower meadow seed mixes. Since they are likely to sneak into the planting anyway, though, they add little value to such a package.

A 1990 survey of the New England Wild Flower Society showed that 7 out of 15 major wildflower meadow seed suppliers supplemented native species with exotics and naturalized aliens in their mixes. Knowing that exotics and naturalized aliens can be over, or under, aggressive, you might be more satisfied in the long run if you plant native species rather than imported European weeds. The Ohio Department of Transportation is trying to do just that.

The problem is finding a commercial source of natives that are indigenous and well adapted to the idiosyncracies of your area. Obviously, large wildflower seedsmen cannot produce native plants from every state in the country. California-based Clyde Robin Seeds, one of the first large meadow mix suppliers, collects seed from around the United States. But they can only harvest seed from those species that thrive in the company's far-western production ranches. The company does its best—albeit imperfectly—to address requests for locally adapted seed. They sell generic, generalized regional mixes for North and South, East and West. For larger orders, they will run a computer simulation of a particular geographic area and custom-blend to match its flora. However, the seed stock may still not be local.

Despite the difficulties involved, there is room for some big gains if more gardeners would explore the virtues of local wildflowers. You can grow a wildflower meadow that is long-lived and conservationally appropriate. And, if you are willing to experiment with species growing in tough sites or not commonly used in commercial mixes, you may just discover unknown garden uses. Although you will not find Ohio wildflowers in a fancy catalog, you can find some species cultivated at Ohio botanical gardens and arboreta, including the Holden Arboretum in Kirtland and Cox Arboretum in Dayton (6733 Springboro Pike, Dayton, 45449; 513-434-9005). You also can dig up and rescue plants from natural sites that are going to be cleared for construction (though caution should be used not to disturb protected varieties). Or collect seed and grow your own, as people used to do just a few decades ago.

CHAPTER SEVEN

A Garden Calendar
for Greater Cleveland

MAINTAINING A REALLY GREAT garden or landscape is considerably easier when regular reminders prompt you to do little jobs around the yard or inspire you to try something fun and different when you have spare time. You'll find some such reminders in the calendar that follows. You can also look for them in newspaper gardening sections, club newsletters, and government agency fliers (see the list at the end of this section). And you can keep your own records. I have done that for the last five years and always chuckle when I go back over some of my old garden records and note interesting similarities—in weather, timing of pests, harvests, and other factors. For instance:

• In each year, snow was predicted for early October. But it only fell at that time in two of those years.
• Drought has struck in August every year except 1992.
• Bean beetles and cabbage loopers swoop into the vegetable garden every July.
• Lettuce and radishes thrive in my cold frame each March.
• I usually find time to finish cleaning up old flower and vegetable stalks in midwinter.

• My large floor plants—a rubber tree and an umbrella tree—get spider mites each February, and need regular showers to keep them healthy until they go outside in May.

• July is usually a disappointment for my annual flowers, which begin to bloom reluctantly; fewer perennials are inclined to flower.

Keeping A Record of Your Garden

When keeping your own garden records, you don't have to be elaborate—just organized. Random notes on scraps of paper can get lost or shuffled out of order and then are impossible to refer to quickly. Instead, try jotting comments in a daily calendar (my favorite method), or on index cards in a monthly file. Make it a practice to come in from the garden, wash your hands, and write down what you have done and observed that day. If you grow certain plants year after year, develop a file on each one, perhaps comparing how different cultivars grow and how they respond to changes in weather or soil. Note when you planted certain plants, when troublesome pests or diseases cropped up, when and why certain plants failed, what new projects you attempted and whether they were successful. These notes, even if they are quite brief, help you build on past successes and avoid repeating past mistakes.

To get you started, or to supplement your existing records, here is a monthly garden calendar of tasks and reminders particular to this region that may occupy your attention over the course of a year.

JANUARY

EARLY JANUARY

❖ Take a break from winter bleakness and visit a greenhouse full of flowers and greenery.

❖ Take some gardening classes or check out a plant society to learn something new to spice up this long winter month.

❖ Start 'Sweet Sandwich' onion seeds indoors under lights; they need to be planted outside extra early in spring to reach a large size. 'Sweet Sandwich' onion bulbs are plenty pungent when you harvest them, but grow mild and sweet after a couple months in storage.

❖ Enjoy the look of plants topped with snow—your own winter wonderland. But be certain that evergreen shrubs growing around the house foundation are protected; heavy wet snow falling off the roof can break them open.

❖ Tune up your lawn mower and sharpen your pruning shears.

❖ Give houseplants a shower to clean the dust off their leaves, bathe them in humidity, and discourage spider mites (which like dry indoor conditions).

❖ Gather some seed catalogs and order something new and better for your garden this coming year. (For a listing of some particularly good seed suppliers, see Other Horticultural Suppliers in chapter 3.)

LATE JANUARY

❖ Watch for a midwinter thaw; use it to plant any spring flowering bulbs you forgot to plant in the fall or to harvest any vegetable crops that remain protected beneath the soil or in a cold frame.

❖ Bring in bulbs that were planted in pots and buried shallow in the garden last fall. Gradually increase the warmth around them to simulate spring and stimulate growth of extra-early flowers.

❖ Take advantage of times when the soil is frozen to finish cleaning up old stems and debris, which can house dormant pests and diseases.

❖ Plant some leaf lettuce, cress, or parsley seed in pots and keep them in a sunny, south-facing window. Eat the greens when they are young; then plant some more.

❖ Buy a flowering houseplant such as clivia, begonias, calla lily, or kalanchoe to cheer up the house.

IDEA FOR JANUARY

How to Keep a Houseplant Alive

If you believe in the green thumb myth, it's time to revolutionize your thinking. Anybody can grow a houseplant. It just takes a little conscientiousness, the right soil, and enough sunlight and water.

The biggest cause of houseplant failure lies in the last category—water. A surprising number of people drown their plants as they smother them with attention. Although the motive may be good, the effect is just as bad as allowing them to die of thirst. The purple thumber keeps on watering without bothering to check if the plant really needs it. The roots start floundering in all the moisture and, as a result, the leaves begin to yellow and wilt. What does this concerned gardener do then? Waters some more. It's a vicious circle.

But there is a simple solution: wait to water until the soil is dry. Stick your finger down in the pot and see if there is water beneath the dry crust on the soil surface. Most plants grown in a peat moss-based mix will be ready for more water before this lower region dries out completely. Others, such as cacti, benefit from getting bone-dry for a short time so their roots can breathe fresh air.

If you don't feel confident making a judgment based on something as unscientific as a finger test, there are other options that are sure-fire. The least expensive is a simple Jobe's Water Spike. These are small tags printed with pictures of watering cans. When the soil dries out, the watering cans turn yellow. Although the package advises using fresh tags every three months, I have used the same ones for years and they are quite reliable.

Or, you can get serious and buy a plant water tester for about $20. These are scientific meters attached to a probe. Insert the probe deep into the pot, and it will rate the wetness or dryness on a scale of varying degrees. Then you can fine-tune the amount you water specifically to each plant. If an African violet, for instance, needs to be watered every time it becomes slightly dry, you'll notice right away.

RECIPE FOR JANUARY

Making Bean Sprouts

Put 2 ounces of sprouting seed (alfalfa, lentils, mung beans, adzuki beans, peas, radishes, sunflowers, or sesame) in a glass canning jar; top with fine nylon mesh secured by the screw-on ring top to hold the seed inside when the jar is tipped upside-down. Use two pieces of mesh, if necessary, to contain smaller seeds. Cover the seeds with lukewarm water and soak over night. Drain the following morning and store the jar in a warm, dark location. Rinse in the evening and twice a day after that, pouring the water off after wetting the seeds. Eat the sprouts when they have emerged and elongated but before they turn green. Store in the refrigerator after seeds have sprouted. Add to sandwiches, salads, soups, or stir-frys.

NOTES

FEBRUARY

EARLY FEBRUARY

❖ Force flowering branches of forsythia to bloom indoors. Cut a few branches that have fat flower buds (sometimes buds are damaged by winter cold) and put them in a vase of water in a fairly cool, humid room. In about two weeks the flowers should open.

❖ Spend a little time planning this year's vegetable garden. Organize it so that each part of the garden will grow crops unrelated to what grew there last year—a technique called crop rotation. By changing the crops grown, you vary the type of nutrients taken from the soil—avoiding depletion—and discourage the buildup of pests and diseases specific to certain kinds of crops. (For more on crop rotation, see my book, *The Harvest Gardener*, 1993, Storey Communications, Pownal, VT.)

❖ Take some time to re-evaluate your landscape. Does it have something of interest to look at in all four seasons? Does it screen off less-than-pleasant views? Are the planted areas in proportion to the house and lot and are they balanced on both sides of the property? If you see room for improvement, sketch your landscape and draw in different plans for how you would revise it. This will give you some good ideas about how to proceed with improvements in spring.

❖ Browse art galleries, garden centers, and catalogs to find a garden sculpture that will give your landscape a focal point all year long.

LATE FEBRUARY

❖ If you have a furry-barked poison ivy vine growing up one of your trees, now's a good time to pull it off. But don't try use your bare hands—it can still give you a rash, even in the dead of winter.

❖ Start pansy seed in a light garden. Put each seed in its own cup of sterile soil-less (peat-based) mix and cover with clear plastic until the seedling has grown several leaves. If you want to grow dozens of pansies, you can start the seed by sprinkling it in a flat (a shallow rectangular nursery container), and transplant the seedlings to individual cups or six-packs when they get to be about two-thirds of an inch tall.

❖ Isolate houseplants that have been attacked by pests so the pests will not spread to other plants. Identify the pest and treat it— nontoxically, if possible. Watch out for:

–Aphids. These sucking insects with soft, pear-shaped bodies spread in great numbers along stems, leaves, buds, and flowers. They excrete sticky honeydew, which often is covered by a dark sooty mold—another easy way to identify these culprits. Kill aphids by blasting them off the plant in the shower or by spraying them with insecticidal soap.

–Mealy bugs. These sucking insects hide under leaves and surround themselves in a shield of cottony-white fluff. You can wash these off with soapy water or use insecticidal soap.

–Spider mites. Tiny (1/50th of an inch) members of the spider family, these mites suck plant juices from the undersides of leaves, making them discolored, speckled, and later brown. Spider mites can spread to infest an entire plant quickly in the dryness indoors. Rinse the plant daily and spray repeatedly with insecticidal soap or pyrethrin.

IDEA FOR FEBRUARY

Hardscape

Architecturally speaking, softscape is a fancy word for the growing, changing, mingling, and merging of plants. They creep, rise up, and spread, giving the landscape a more comfortable, gentle look. They delight us with their varying images, textures, fragrances, and fruits.

Hardscapes, on the other hand, look the same all the time. These are permanent structures such as walks, patios, decks, and raised retaining walls. They stalwartly provide structure and lines, angles and curves, through dreary winter, baking summer, and unexpected frosts. Hardscape may not be alive, but at least it is consistent.

Make a note to re-evaluate your hardscape. Does it look as good as the lawn, flower gardens, and shade trees? Or is there a cracking cement walk that angles stiffly and abruptly up to the brickwork of your house? Maybe this would be a good time to think about exchanging it for a slightly curved brick walk. Is that corroding deck too small to hold all the grandchildren at family get-togethers? Perhaps it is time to pave a larger space of stone, brick, tiles, or interlocking pavers.

Improvements to the hardscape will last for years. Take plenty of time now to determine what building material and structure will look and work best. Schedule a qualified contractor or landscaper (see Landscape Specialists, chapter 3), or save labor costs if you have the time and skill to do the job yourself. Either way, insist on top-quality workmanship, or the entire landscape will suffer.

Two useful books full of ideas and plans for hardscape projects are: *Stonescaping*, by Jan Kowalczewski Whitner, and *Step By Stem Outdoor Brickwork*, by David Holloway (both from Gardenway Publishing, Storey Communications, Pownal, VT).

RECIPE FOR FEBRUARY

Fragrant Potpourri from Scented Geraniums
Scented geraniums are smaller flowered relatives of the annual bedding geranium that have foliage delightfully scented with rose, apple, lemon, mint, pine, or other fragrances.

Many people who grow scented geraniums cut the greenery back in early October and keep the plants indoors during winter. If the plant grows in a light garden or bright window, it will have resprouted, often growing quite large by February. A wonderful fragrant potpourri can be made from the leaves of these flowers.

Harvest individual leaves and dry them in a dehydrator or microwave (see the operating manual for instructions) until they are crackly crisp. Put one cup of the dried leaves in an small open bowl or basket.

Mix sweetly scented dried leaves with a half cup of colorful or fragrant plant products, such as dried flower petals, everlasting flowers, lavender, and dried lemon or orange peel.

If you have a more pungent type of scented geranium, try a half cup of small hemlock cones, pine needles, cedar chips, or pine-scented rosemary, with some flower petals for color.

Stir or heat slightly to release the fragrance. Replace as soon as the fragrance diminishes, or replenish with a few drops of your favorite essential oil, many kinds of which are available in craft and florist shops.

NOTES

MARCH

EARLY MARCH

❖ Prune deciduous trees and shrubs. Shape them by cutting off overly long or dead limbs and branches that cross, rub, or shade another.

❖ Wait to prune spring flowering shrubs until after they flower. Also, wait until summer to prune maples and birches, which leak sap from spring pruning cuts. The sap does not damage the tree but certainly looks unpleasant.

❖ Start cool season crops such as cabbage, broccoli, lettuce, parsley, sweet alyssum, and calendula for planting outside in late April.

❖ Pot tender tubers (which do not survive frost), such as tuberous begonias, elephant's-ears (*Caladium*), tuberose, and calla lilies. Keep them in a sunny location indoors until the danger of frost passes.

❖ Enjoy the maple syrup produced by the many sugar maples in our area. Learn how to tap your own trees.

❖ Find out how fertile your soil is: have it tested by the County Cooperative Extension Service. Call to receive a test packet (Cuyahoga: 631-1890, Geauga: 834-4656, Lake: 357-2582, Lorain: 322-0127, Medina: 725-4911, Summit: 497-1611).

LATE MARCH

❖ If you want to save money on new plants and experiment with new and different cultivars, you can start eggplant, tomato, and pepper seeds indoors under lights. Also try perennial coneflowers, flax, English daisies, columbine, Shasta daisies, petunias, and salvia from seed.

❖ Watch for the tiny flowers on maples, oaks, and other deciduous trees. They create a blushing halo around the leafless trees, and are especially lovely to see—a cascade of color—when you view a woodland hillside from afar (for example, the Cuyahoga Valley National Recreation Center area from I-271).

❖ There is often a dry spell during this month when you can begin preparing the soil for flower or vegetable gardens or for new landscape beds—even when it is still too cold to start planting. If you need to order topsoil, do it now if conditions are dry. Landscapers are not as busy as they will be later in the season, so you may be able to get some help fast.

❖ When the weather is dry but cool, you can do hardscape work, such as building a rock garden, a rock retaining wall, a brick walk, or patio. Any construction must be completed before you can safely plant around the area—first things first!

❖ Look for areas with poor drainage. These are easy to spot after the snow melts because water puddles there. Since most plants can't grow in saturated soil, raise the lawn or garden with more topsoil and route the excess water out of the yard with a drainage ditch or underground drainage tiles.

❖ If you order a truckload of topsoil to raise an area, look for soil that is premixed with organic matter like leaf compost or decayed horse manure. This is fluffier and more fertile than plain clay topsoil and makes growing ornamentals or turf easier.

IDEA FOR MARCH

Proper Pruning

There are some new thoughts on the best way to prune naturally. Because early spring is an ideal time to prune shrubs and trees (except leaky maples and birches and flowering shrubs), here is something to ponder as you clean and sharpen your pruning tools.

The idea behind natural pruning is to use a plant's growth habits to your advantage; it makes the pruning job easier and your landscape more attractive. Shrubs will flow into clusters or masses that blend into natural-looking screens, backdrops, and islands of interest.

On the other hand, when you shear an evergreen into a box or barrel shape you set it apart from the rest of your yard. And you make more work for yourself. When you clip with hedge shears, you leave stubs above the slightly swollen nodes where leaves, twigs, and buds arise. This interrupts normal growth patterns and encourages many new shoots to race for the sun. The cluster of young shoots will need shearing again very soon. And the shrub will become a shell of greenery with a barren interior.

If instead of shearing you would thin out long, weak, or undesirable branches one at a time by cutting back to a node, you could prune just once a year and maintain the soft, natural shape of the shrub. The process is simple but requires you to deal with individual branches. Use hand-held pruning shears to cut off overcrowded twigs, long-handled loppers for branches between an inch and two inches in diameter, and a pruning saw for larger limbs. (Save hedge shears for hedges.) If a branch is too tall, cut it back to a side branch that is at least two-thirds of its diameter, or remove the branch where it emerges at the ground. A new shoot will take its place, keeping the plant young as well as short.

It's hard to begin this kind of thinning on an evergreen that has already been sheared. You can renovate some healthy broadleaf evergreens by cutting off one-third of the oldest branches every year and thinning the new ones that take their place. In three years, the shrub will look like new. Narrow-leaf evergreens such as junipers and yews will not resprout from wood that has no greenery. Either cut them back to actively growing shoots or remove very old branches entirely.

On trees, remove damaged branches or limbs that hang too low or rub each other or the house. Call an arborist if the branches are large and heavy, or are located anywhere near power lines. For smaller branches that you can handle yourself, cut outside the swollen branch collar that connects the branch to the trunk or parent limb. Don't cut flush with the branch; this leaves a larger wound and removes the collar, a powerhouse of chemicals that seal off the rest of the tree from pests and diseases. First, cut upward from the bottom of the branch until the saw reaches about one-third of the way through. Finish the cut from the top, placing it just outside the first cut. This allows the branch to fall without tearing healthy bark on the trunk.

For more on pruning, see *All About Pruning* (1989, Ortho Books, San Francisco, CA), which I co-wrote with Fred Buscher, professor emeritus at Ohio State University.

Recipe for March

String Bean Casserole
This is a good time to use up the rest of the beans you froze from last year's garden. Try them in this casserole, which is reprinted with permission from *Nature Center Cookery* (edited by Kathy Heffernan and Carol Provan, 1981, Shaker Lakes Regional Nature Center).

  1/4 cup flour
  2 cups milk
  1 cup cream
  1/8 teaspoon hot pepper sauce

3/4 pound American cheese

4 teaspoons soy sauce

1 teaspoon salt

1/2 teaspoon pepper

3–4 packages (10 ounces each) frozen French-style string
    beans, thawed and drained

2 cans (4 1/2 ounces each) mushrooms

1/2 cup onions, minced

2 tablespoons butter

1 can (8 ounces) water chestnuts, halved

3/4 cup almonds

1/2 cup bread crumbs

Mix together the flour, milk, cream, hot pepper sauce, cheese, soy sauce, salt, and pepper. Add the string beans and mushrooms. Sauté the onions in the butter. Add to bean mixture. Add the water chestnuts. Place in buttered 3-quart casserole.

Mix almonds and bread crumbs, and sprinkle over casserole. Dot with butter. Bake at 350°F for 40 to 45 minutes. Yield: 10 servings.

Note: for an interesting flavor variation, cook the beans with 1 1/2 teaspoons of savory (either summer or winter).

Notes

April

Early April

❖ Look for wildflowers, such as coltsfoot, blooming along the roadways on warm days. Forsythias also are coming along now.

❖ Spring flowering bulbs are coming up. Leave their foliage on until it yellows to recharge the bulb with energy so it will perform well next year.

❖ Sow seeds of leaf lettuce, spinach, Swiss chard, arugula, parsley, and radishes outdoors every two weeks during spring for plenty of fresh salads before summer heat sets in. Protect the young plants under a floating row cover. The first crop may or may not thrive, depending on the weather, but will be wonderful if it does. The next succession you plant is sure to succeed.

❖ Invest in a cold frame or make your own. This is a large box (6 to 12 inches high in the front, 12 to 18 inches high in the rear). Top it with a clear, sloping lid (which will catch the sun's rays most efficiently) that you can open for access and ventilation. To make your own, build the box of wood or cement blocks, and the lid of an old glass window. Use it to grow perennials, hardy herbs, lettuce, endive, and pansies from seed.

You can also protect early crops with low plastic tunnels, hot caps, Wall O' Water protectors, or similar translucent-walled insulating structures.

Late April

❖ You may be receiving bare rootstock from catalog orders now—perennials, strawberries, and roses that are grown in fields and then dug, freed of soil, and shipped directly to you while they are still dormant. Plant these outside in a prepared bed as soon your shipment arrives. Or transplant them into a large nursery container and keep them in a protected outdoor location until you can get a garden area ready.

❖ Start peas early if you have a raised bed that is warmer and drier than the surrounding soil. (If the soil is too cold and wet, the seed will rot.) You can pre-sprout the seed in peat pots indoors and set the small seedlings out under floating row covers (and plastic in severe weather).

❖ New shrubs and trees will be arriving at nearby garden centers. This is a good time to browse around and pick out the choice plants that will enhance your landscape.

❖ If you want to plant vegetables extra early, lay a sheet of clear or green infrared transmitting (IRT) plastic (a new type of plastic developed to warm soil up fast) on the soil for several weeks before your anticipated planting date. Both types intensify sun warmth; only the green blocks weed growth.

❖ Apply a lawn fertilizer containing slow-release nitrogen now. This causes less pollution from fertilizer run off, encourages the grass to grow slightly slower, and needs to be applied only once a year.

❖ Plant grass seed on new lawns or on bare spots in existing lawns, taking advantage of spring rains and leafless trees to provide young grasses with extra water and light.

❖ Start seeds of cucumbers, melons, squash and pumpkins, marigolds, basil, and nasturtiums in peat pots indoors in a light garden or a sunny south-facing window. You can transplant them outdoors after the last frost.

❖ If your yard is so shady that few plants grow well, this is a good time to call an arborist and have your shade trees limbed up (the lower limbs removed), or thinned (some of the branches removed to let filtered light through). You might even remove a few trees altogether.

Idea for April

Gardening in Containers

Sometimes the most successful garden is the smallest one, especially if it's grown in a container. Making a garden in a pot or planter puts you in the driver's seat. You will control elements of nature's domain, variables such as soil, water, nutrients, and even sunlight. Set a concrete planter in a sunny gap in a shady yard; put a plastic-lined peach basket on the balcony of an apartment; edge a patio with open-end-up clay drain tiles of various heights. Or invest in redwood window boxes or similar containers made of long-lasting fiberglass.

Whether you spend a bundle or nothing on a container, remember these tips:

• Wood inevitably will rot, but redwood, cedar, and pressure-treated lumber last longest.

• Fiberglass may crack.

• Clay and terra-cotta pots will also crack, especially if you leave them outside in the winter.

• Ornamental vases may lack drainage holes. Put a layer of stones in the bottom and water carefully so the plants don't drown.

• Metal containers transmit winter cold and summer heat. To moderate both extremes, line the container with a layer of plastic foam.

Fill your planter with a good soil, usually a soil-less professional mix rather than potting soil, which will pack too densely for good root growth. Allow plenty of rooting depth or the plant is likely to fade in midsummer. Fertilize regularly with a diluted, balanced, water-soluble fertilizer.

Your plants will need extra water—as often as twice a day if you put smaller pots out in summer sun and heat. You'll also find that porous clay pots dry out faster than plastic or metal. To slow water loss, add a water-holding gel (see Proper Planting, chapter 6) to the soil and grow drought-tolerant plants such as ageratum, cockscomb, marigold, geranium, and portulaca. Or double-pot: put one pot inside a larger one and fill the gap between with moist peat moss or vermiculite. Or buy a planter that is set above a reservoir of water that is pulled up into the pot with a wick.

RECIPE FOR APRIL

Spicy Mesclun Salad

Grow the following greens in spring and snip off the tender young leaves when they are about two inches long.

> 4 cups assorted leaf lettuce, including one kind with red leaves
>
> 2/3 cup French sorrel
>
> 2/3 cup arugula
>
> 2/3 cup Mizuna Japanese parsley

Wash and dry greens. Add 1/2 cup radish seedpods, halved. (Harvest them from radish plants that have flowered and set seedpods that are beginning to swell.) Serve with vinegar and oil dressing to taste. Yield: 4 servings.

NOTES

MAY

EARLY MAY

❖ Wildflowers are going strong; take a walk through the Metro-parks to enjoy them and consider planting some of the showier ones—such as liverwort, jack-in-the-pulpit, Dutchman's-breeches, and wild geranium—in your garden. For more information, see *Wildflowers* (by Rick Imes, 1993, Rodale Press, Emmaus, PA).

❖ Take note of which trees and shrubs are in flower simultaneously and surround them with complementary bulbs, perennials, and bedding flowers.

❖ Weeds will be growing quickly at this time of year. Be sure to hoe or pull every one out so they cannot reproduce. If you clean out garden weeds early in the season, you will not have to weed as much later in the summer, fall, and following year.

❖ A frost may still strike just when flowering trees and shrubs are at their peak. If it does, cover small trees and shrubs with plastic, burlap, or paper to protect their flowers.

❖ If you want to have more of a particular kind of perennial flower, or if you want to shuffle a perennial to a different part of the garden, dig and divide now while the shoots are emerging from the ground. You can divide nearly any species now except spring blooming plants, which are best divided when they fall dormant in summer or fall, or plants that resent disturbance, such as peonies, monkshood, and gas plant.

❖ Watch for borers on bearded irises. If you have a problem with them, spray from the time the eggs hatch in spring, suggests Dorothy Willott, a breeder in Beachwood. If you find the off-color trails borers make in the foliage, follow them and squash the wormlike borer when you find it. Cut off the flower stalks after blooming so borers can't tunnel down them and bore into the rhizomes.

❖ Support floppy perennials such as certain peonies, Shasta daisies, and asters with wire grid supports. Plants can grow up through these grids and then fill out to hide the wire. For perennials with long stems and large flowers, such as delphinium and dahlias, tie the rising stems to green bamboo stakes. If you wait until the plants are flopping, you may break the stems or destroy the natural character of the plant by forcing it upright in a corset of twine.

LATE MAY

❖ Take out some books or attend classes on basic flower arranging so you can use the flowers you grow to decorate your dining room table.

❖ Plant potatoes and corn a couple weeks before the last frost date—they can take a slight chill, and with an early start they sometimes escape attacks by pests like Colorado potato beetles and aphids.

❖ After the last frost date, plant tender crops such as bedding annuals (marigolds, ageratum, petunias, zinnias), vegetable plants (tomatoes, peppers, eggplants), vegetable seeds (beans, cucumbers, squash), and annual herbs (basil, sweet marjoram, summer savory).

❖ Harvest asparagus while the heads are still tight and before the spears get long and tough.

❖ Take houseplants outdoors to a shady location for the summer. Most perk up dramatically given this extra sunlight and drenching rain. Remember to remove the drainage pan beneath the pot so rainwater can drain freely.

Idea for May

Be Sure Soil Is Dry Enough Before You Start to Work

Since most of the soil in these parts is a stiff clay (see Dealing With Clay, chapter 6), it tends to stay wet well into the planting season. Wet soil is not only difficult and mucky to work in, it is also vulnerable to compression. Even though you are brave enough to enter a mud pit of a garden, you could do serious damage to the soil. Wait to till the earth or to do a lot of walking in your garden until a ball of soil breaks easily in your fist. Any earlier and you may have a garden of bricks rather than plants.

If you want to be able to get into a garden earlier in spring, raise it 6 to 12 inches above the surrounding soil, so the water will drain off. And amend it with sharp sand and compost, which loosen the soil and let water escape.

Recipe for May

Super Savory Sugar Snap Peas

Sugar snap peas, which are eaten pod and all, are extra delicious if you eat them just moments after picking. The best sugar snaps contain peas that are swollen, but not full-sized, in a glossy-skinned pod; these are at their sweetest. Try them in this easy recipe.

    3 tablespoons butter or margarine
    1 teaspoon fresh summer savory, chopped
    1 pint sugar snap peas

Sauté one teaspoon finely chopped summer savory in 3

tablespoons butter over medium heat. When the savory has wilted, set the pan aside for 15 minutes to let the flavors steep. Go outdoors and harvest a pint of prime sugar snap peas. Rinse them, and remove strings and tops. Sauté the pods in the savory butter for two minutes, stirring once. Eat immediately. Yield: 4 servings.

NOTES

June

Early June

❖ Rhododendrons are just finishing their prime-time bloom. Visit some rhododendron gardens and nurseries—but remember that rhododendrons need well-drained soil. Don't bother to plant them unless you are willing to create the proper conditions.

❖ Strawberries are at their peak. Keep a close eye on your own, or on the pick-your-own strawberry farms, so you can harvest them when they are perfectly ripe. These strawberries are sweeter (and more perishable) than anything you buy at a store.

❖ Old-fashioned roses are at their peak of bloom. Look in rose display gardens and at nurseries for some of the roses that fashioned history.

❖ Get in the habit of weeding and hoeing once a week or more, because the weeds will be rocketing up. If you can get rid of weeds before they set seed, you'll eliminate most of your weed problem.

❖ If you hate to stake perennials upright but also dislike how some droop when in flower, consider placing a self-supporting plant nearby for the droopers to lean on. For instance, you could put droopy frikart's asters next to sturdy boltonia, or droopy red yarrow near sturdy iris leaves.

Late June

❖ Cabbage loopers (green caterpillars spawned by the small white moths that flutter around vegetable gardens) will demolish broccoli, cabbage, Chinese cabbage, and cauliflower plants if you're not alert. Spray with Bt (a bacterial disease of caterpillars) to control them without using poisons.

❖ Those cute little baby bunnies you saw in spring are getting bigger, and so is their appetite for anything green. Encourage them to leave by cleaning up their hiding places—old sheds, log piles, weedy corners—and fencing in your vegetable garden. Use a fine wire mesh fence about three feet high and buried at least six inches below the ground so they cannot tunnel under.

❖ If you usually have problems with insect pests, you could try buying an army of beneficial insects from a mail-order insect farm. (There are many of these nationwide; you can find their catalogs in the library of The Garden Center of Greater Cleveland.) Beneficial insects prey on, or parasitize, pests—there are dozens of them to choose from. Ladybugs are one kind that lives naturally around here, though they are not worth ordering, because they will just fly away. Other types, though, such as spined soldier bugs (for beetles and other pests), mealybug destroyers, fly parasites, and tiny parasitic wasps that attack caterpillars can do a good job. The best bugs tend to get sold out fast, so order early.

❖ Deadhead perennials (remove the faded blooms) to give the plants energy and vigor they would otherwise have spent in seed production. Cut off the old flowers individually if more buds remain ready to bloom, or cut off the whole stalk at the base if the flowers are gone for the season. Plants such as yarrow, Shasta daisies, delphinium, and coreopsis usually rebloom after deadheading.

❖ Plant more bean seed so you have fresh beans all summer long. Inoculate the seed or the trenches you set the seed in with powder-like, nitrogen-fixing bacteria, often sold as legume inoculant. These bacteria help beans, peas, and other legumes grow by pulling nitrogen out of the air and fixing it in a form plants can use. Once you apply inoculant, the bacteria will stay in the soil for years.

IDEA FOR JUNE

Edibles Can Be Ornamental, Too

Your garden can look as good as it tastes. If you're short on space, time, energy, or enthusiasm, conserve your resources by planting ornamental edibles.

One of my favorites, which you can plant now, is red-stemmed Swiss chard, a salad green that's also good for steaming. It grows in upright clumps, an interesting variation when planted among annual bedding flowers. If you complement its red stalks with low-growing annual flowers such as pink petunias or blue pansies, the effect is stunning.

Other vegetables are earning a place in flower gardens. Pepper plants, especially bred to be compact and bear yellow, orange, red, and purple upright pods, are popular for edging or using in masses. Use ornamental cabbages and kale, with blue, white, pink, purple, and blue foliage, for a lovely fall display. Kale usually will stay pretty until late into December. (But don't forget to control cabbage looper caterpillars or they will deform the showy head.)

Some flowers are also edible. Peppery-flavored nasturtium flowers, leaves, and seeds are wonderful in salads or herbal vinegars. Calendula, or pot marigold, which you can plant now or in the late summer, has an interesting bitter flavor. Don't forget sunflowers, which are available in a two-foot-tall form—wonderful for small sunny spaces.

Take caution, though: when you mix ornamentals and edibles, don't spray herbicides, fungicides, or pesticides that are not safe to eat.

RECIPE FOR JUNE

Basil Bean Salad
1 pound French-cut green beans
1 large onion, sliced thin
5 tablespoons olive oil
3 tablespoons vinegar
pinch of dry mustard
1/4 teaspoon dry basil
salt and pepper to taste
3 tablespoons sugar

Place cooked beans in a serving container. Add onion. In a small bowl, combine oil, vinegar, mustard, basil, salt, pepper, and sugar until well blended. Pour dressing over beans and onions and toss gently. This is best made the day before serving. Yield: 4 servings.

Adapted from *Nature Center Cookery* (edited by Kathy Heffernan and Carol Provan, 1981, Shaker Lakes Regional Nature Center).

NOTES

July

Early July

❖ If the weather is dry, red spider mites may show up on mums, roses, cucumbers, annuals, delphiniums, phlox, and even some shrubs and trees. As soon as you detect their presence, call a horticultural hotline to find out how to take preventive action. (See Other Answer Sources, chapter 2.)

❖ Annual flowers may begin to slow down after their first riotous burst of bloom. Cut them back by about one-third, then water and fertilize to rejuvenate them.

❖ Mulch your vegetable garden with straw to keep the soil moister and cooler. You can also mulch your trees and shrubs, but don't layer shredded bark on too thickly.

❖ You may have the pleasure of picking your first zucchini and beans now. They will be succulent and delightful. Keep harvesting both crops; if the pods or squash mature on the vine, they will stop producing new edibles.

❖ Keep pulling out crops that have finished producing, as well as the weeds. Compost them all, as long as they do not carry seeds or diseases. Some disease spores and weed seeds will survive despite the composting process and attack again when you use the compost.

❖ Fewer perennial flowers bloom at this time of year, so the perennial garden may be looking a bit shabby. Clean up the flowers that have already bloomed by cutting back faded blossoms. Then find room for several clumps of a plant that will bring color to the midsummer garden, such as coneflower, 'Moonbeam' threadleaf coreopsis, late Shasta daisies, balloon flower (*Platycodon grandiflorus*), or speedwell (*Veronica spicata*).

LATE JULY

❖ Even though the weather is getting hot, you can still plant container-grown shrubs, trees, and perennials. Just be sure to keep the area moist for the next three or four weeks.

❖ Look into lighting your garden so you can enjoy it more at night. You can install lights along a walk, near the patio, or on a specimen tree to show it off like a piece of art.

❖ Beans, squash, and even a few tomatoes will begin ripening. Make a point to pull out a few recipes that feature these crops so you can make the most of them.

❖ If Japanese beetles become a problem, treat your lawn with milky spore disease, which, in a few years, will kill beetle grubs as they emerge from underground. Don't bother with Japanese beetle traps—they may attract more beetles than they capture.

❖ Wouldn't a water garden with water lilies, fish, or a trickling waterfall be soothing right now? You can make a small water garden in a plastic-lined half barrel, antique bathtub, horse trough, or other deep watertight container to see if you like gardening with aquatic plants. If all goes well, you can expand to an in-ground water garden next year.

IDEA FOR JULY

Give Perennials Some Attention

In springtime, perennial flower gardens are like a beautiful tapestry of colors and textures. But in summer, many a garden begins to fray. When springtime bloom is through, you will be left with barren stems and browning pods. Don't worry. Just get out your pruning shears and start trimming.

Many plants suffer in midsummer, but perennial gardens are most notorious for their bleakness. Once they are through flowering, they channel all their remaining energy into seed production, a wasted effort from most gardeners' perspectives. Get rid of those seed heads and you'll benefit twice. Plants will look much neater and some will put out another small show of flowers.

Before cutting, look at the flowering stem of your perennial flowers. Some are simply a stalk with all the flowers at the summit. When these are done blooming, shear off all the stems. This may bring about a second bloom in plants such as sea pinks and coralbells.

On perennials such as phlox, Shasta daisies, yarrow, and delphinium, old brown flower clusters are noticeable at the top. But at the junction of leaf sets below, there may lie a small cluster of flower buds waiting for an opportunity to sprout. Cut off the old flowers and let the new take their place. This type of pruning takes a little more time and care, but it's worth the trouble. When the stem is finally through blooming, it may begin to yellow. This is the time to cut it out entirely at the base.

Some perennials, such as Shasta daisies, lobelia, and mountain bluet, revert to a low-growing rosette form for winter. It's natural for all tall stems to die back as the plant reverts to this state; remove the old stems when you see the rosette is established. Other perennials, like peonies, maintain attractive foliage long after flowers are gone. Cut off these seed heads so that plants use all their energy for good health and growth rather than seed production.

A few perennial flowers look good with seed heads attached. Astilbe, butterfly weed, coneflowers, *Sedum* 'Autumn Joy', and ornamental grasses are just a few. Leave the pods and capsules on these unless the plant seems to be suffering.

Others, such as columbine, bellflower, and violets, produce

seed that is worth keeping. You might let these seed heads stay to maturity and sprinkle their offspring through the bed.

RECIPE FOR JULY

Yellow Squash with Fresh Thyme
   When you have a lot of squash coming in from the garden, try some innovative ways of serving it to make the rich garden-fresh flavor a treat. Here's one of my favorites.

   1 tablespoon butter
   1 teaspoon fresh thyme leaves
   4 young yellow squash, sliced
   salt and freshly ground black pepper, to taste

   Melt the butter with the thyme in a large skillet over medium-low heat. Add the squash, stirring to mix well. Cook covered, stirring occasionally for 5 minutes. Season with salt and pepper to taste. Yield: 4 servings
   (From my book, *The Harvest Gardener*, 1993, Storey Communications, Pownal, VT.)

NOTES

August

Early August

❖ Because we often have a drought in midsummer, prepare for the worst. Use leaky hoses or trickle-irrigation to provide water slowly at ground level. This minimizes water loss to evaporation and discourages leaf diseases, such as black spot, which get started on wet foliage.

❖ If you cannot keep your lawn watered, it may turn brown. Fortunately, grasses are capable of going dormant during stressful times. Unless the drought is prolonged, they will green up again in fall (or when rain resumes).

❖ Plan a picnic now because you won't have to mow as often.

❖ If you see that trees and shrubs (especially newly planted ones) are struggling in dry conditions, let a hose trickle on them for up to several hours at a time. It should soak the soil deeply so that tree roots will continue to dig deeper and stay moist for some time.

❖ Humidity is often high even during our usual August droughts. Expect to see an increase in plant diseases such as mildew on roses, phlox, zinnias, asters, lilacs, and bee balm. You can prevent mildew with protective sprays of fungicides, but only if you're persistent. Or look for disease-resistant forms of these plants—they're out there if you're willing to search.

❖ Replant some fall crops, such as lettuce, radishes, and beets, in the shade of tomatoes and beans. The shade will help them get started in the heat; then you can pull out the faded tomato or bean plant to give the fall crops full sun.

❖ Move and divide summer-dormant perennials such as iris, Oriental poppy, Virginia bluebells, and bleeding heart.

LATE AUGUST

❖ This is a good time to pick and dry herbs and flowers. Herbs dry best in a dehydrator or near a dehumidifier or air conditioner. They often mildew if left out in high humidity. Everlasting flowers, including strawflowers and statice, dry much more easily; just hang them in an airy dark closet. Other flowers—roses, for example—will dry if you work them into a sealed container of desiccant such as silica gel.

❖ Stop pruning hardy trees and shrubs (with the exception of hybrid tea roses). Pruning now could stimulate them to put out new growth, which will not be hardened enough to survive winter.

❖ Give hybrid tea roses their last dose of fertilizer so they can begin to wind down before cold weather comes.

IDEA FOR AUGUST

Plants that Tolerate Drought

As August clouds roll over my garden without dropping a single hint of moisture, the sugar maple foliage begins to droop. The leather-leaf viburnums become tinted with autumn red and the sweet woodruff wilts flat on the ground. The lawn falls dormant and turns brown.

Since drought can be expected nearly every summer, we need to identify which plants require special attention when rainfall is scarce and which can hold their own. Most plants that we commonly grow, especially bluegrass, vegetables, and roses, require one inch of rainfall per week. If moisture does not come naturally, it must be provided through irrigation (if there is not a watering ban in the area).

Soak the soil deeply, encouraging the roots to dig down where they will have access to more moisture. Try to avoid watering by hand, especially trees and shrubs; most of us just don't have the patience to stand there holding the hose long enough to wet soil thoroughly. And sprinkling is not particularly efficient either. Most of that moisture evaporates into the air from leaf surfaces or goes to feeding weeds between plants. The best option is a trickle system. This delivers moisture directly to plant roots. Simply run a small stream of water out of a hose onto tree roots, or buy a canvas or perforated plastic hose that will release gentle droplets of water. You can also invest in a permanent underground irrigation system.

To minimize the garden's dependence on water, plant species that can go for long spells without rain. They may develop deep root systems; they may store water in leaves, stems, or roots; or they may protect their foliage from water loss with waxy, leathery, bristly, or hairy coatings. Some even vary their method of photosynthesis to minimize water loss through leaf pores. Here's a shopping list of plants that will tolerate future droughts:

- Annual flowers: Annual phlox, portulaca, California poppy, morning glory, annual pinks
- Perennial flowers: Yarrow, yellow and purple coneflowers, perennial sunflowers, blanketflower, coreopsis, daylilies, hosta, sedums, sweet William, Oriental poppies
- Herbs: Perennial thyme, rosemary, sage, savory, oregano, santolina
- Vegetables: Swiss chard, purslane, Good-King-Henry, sorrel
- Shrubs: Junipers, Japanese and Mentor barberry, flowering quince, smoke tree, privet, potentilla, Amur maple, Russian olive, witch hazel, St.-John's-wort, Nannyberry viburnum, yucca, staghorn sumac, buckthorn
- Trees: Osage orange, juniper, golden-rain tree, bur oak, locust, sassafras, Siberian elm

Recipe for August

Tomato-Onion Pie
  8 medium onions, peeled and sliced
  5 cups soft bread cubes
  8 medium-size tomatoes, peeled and sliced
  1 tablespoon sugar
  1/2 teaspoon salt
  1/8 teaspoon freshly ground black pepper
  2 tablespoons butter or margarine

  Preheat oven to 350°F Boil onions in 1/2 cup salted water until they are almost tender. Drain. Heavily butter a 2-quart casserole dish. Line the bottom of the dish with 4 cups of the bread cubes, reserving 1 cup for topping. Layer onions and tomatoes over bread cubes. Sprinkle sugar, salt, and pepper over tomatoes. Top with reserved bread cubes. Dot with butter. Bake in a preheated oven for about 30 minutes. Yield: 8 to 10 servings.
  (From my book, *The Harvest Gardener*, 1993, Storey Communications, Pownal, VT.)

Notes

September

Early September

❖ Use some dried herbs and garden flowers, plus wild roadside flowers to make everlasting wreaths. Wire small bunches of flowers and herb sprigs onto a framework of wire, grapevines, or straw, all of which are available at most florists.

❖ Plant some evergreens to screen out unpleasant views, muffle traffic sounds, or give a view of solid greenery this winter. Look for conifers that are not sheared for a more natural look. Keep new plantings moist through the fall.

❖ Sow seeds of hardy annuals such as sweet alyssum, pansies, Shirley and California poppies. These can pass the winter while quite small and will flower very early next year.

❖ Plant cold-tolerant greens such as spinach, endive, and winter lettuces like 'Arctic King', 'Brune d'Hiver', and 'Winter Density'. Grow them to a small size in a well drained bed and cover with a floating row cover and straw when the weather turns cold in November or December. They will stay small during winter and begin growing extra early in spring.

❖ Buy some ornamental kale plants for your garden. These colorful-leaved plants will stay beautiful well into December.

Late September

❖ Prepare houseplants to return indoors. Evict crawling bugs that have crept into the drainage holes in the bottom of the pot and any pests on the leaves or stems. Move the plants gradually into dimmer, warmer locations until they are acclimated to household conditions. Once indoors, they will begin a period of rest and need less water and little fertilizer.

❖ Look for some late crops to be abundant now, such as bush lima beans, hot peppers, and eggplants. You can freeze eggplant after dipping peeled slices in egg, then breading and baking. Roast, dry, or pickle hot peppers.

❖ Garden chores slow down a bit at this time. If you've been planning to put in a new garden bed, this is a good time to do so. Since nursery stock often is picked over at this time of year, you may have to wait until spring to find the best cultivars and specimens.

❖ Admire wild goldenrod and purple New England asters that spread across meadows and roadways all around town. You can move some of these wild prairie plants into large gardens or naturalized areas near your home so you are sure to have lots of fall color.

Idea for September

Choreographing Bulbs

Are you planting more bulbs and enjoying them less? It may be difficult to imagine a less-than-attractive daffodil or tulip, but colors mixed unknowingly can look polka-dotted and chaotic. Be certain any investment you make in bulbs and planting time is well spent. Study what is available at garden centers. Pick different types of bulbs that will come into and go out of flower the entire spring season.

Henk Koster, chief garden architect of the Dutch Keukenhof Garden where millions of bulbs are put on display from February to June, explained the concept. "It's like dance choreography," he said. "You plan blooming so that everything happens when you want it to, in sequence. It's also important to consider the blooming times of flowering shrubs and other perennials."

Furthermore, plan to blend handsome color combinations that look good with other bulbs, as well as your landscape and home. "Color is really the key," Koster said. "Bulbs are color. If you put masses of color together, you achieve a more stunning effect."

Ellen Henke, California-based botanist and gardening spokesperson, writes in *Flower and Garden* about techniques she uses to create movement. She combines no fewer than 12 bulbs of a single cultivar into a mass, not a straight line. She puts the tall bulbs in a triangle toward the back of the bed and matches their color to shorter bulbs in the front. The color flows back and forth, side to side. You also can match bulb colors with low-growing perennials or annuals such as violas, pansies, English daisies, or forget-me-nots.

Once you have the color coordinated, pay attention to smaller details: flower shapes, foliage colors, and the overall form of the plant. "What makes a planting impressive from a distance might be sharp contrasts of color or patterns of contrasting or complementary colors," Koster said. "Up close, the shape and textures of the flowers and leaves become important." You might consider using varied flower types, such as lily-flowered tulips or double-flowering daffodils, or species tulips that have interesting patterns on their leaves.

RECIPE FOR SEPTEMBER

Harvesting and Drying Herbs for Teas
1. Be sure that sprays and pesticides have not been used.
2. Pick plant materials on a sunny day, ideally after two consecutive days of sunshine. The flavor will be stronger.
3. Discover the prime time for each plant. Usually this is just before flowers form. When herb flowers are used, pick them in bud or early bloom.
4. Immediately after picking, wash plant material in lukewarm water. Use a large container filled with water. Change

water three or four times for a thorough cleaning. When clean, place herbs in a terry towel and gently pat dry.

5. Dry herbs on screens in an area away from light and where air circulates. Dry until *crisp*.

6. Before drying scented geranium or large basil leaves, use scissors to remove the large center vein in each leaf.

7. Strip dried leaves from stems before storing. For evenly dried leaves, place in a shallow pan and put in a warm oven (150°F) for up to 10 minutes. Keep oven door slightly open.

8. To create tea blends, rub the leaves through a coarse sieve. A food processor may also be used to crumble herb leaves; use quick on/off pulses to achieve uniformity. Guard against over-processing or powdering the leaves.

9. Store material in glass jars, tightly capped, in a dark, cool cupboard. Label and date the containers. Refresh supply each year.

Note: Follow these same steps for harvesting and drying herbs for culinary uses.

(Reprinted with permission from *Cooking With Herb Scents*, edited by Donna Agan, 1991, the Western Reserve Herb Society.)

NOTES

OCTOBER

EARLY OCTOBER

❖ Harvest pumpkins and squash before they are hit by frost or sit on the wet soil too long. In either case, they will not keep very long. Store them at about 50°F, if possible, for the longest shelf life.

❖ Plant fall bulbs. Make groups of the same varieties, five, seven, or more per group. These larger bunches of flowers provide more impact when seen from a distance. (See Choreographing Bulbs in the September section for more details.)

❖ Put extra bulbs into flowerpots, sink them in holes in the garden, and surround the pots with sand. Give them from 8 to 15 months outdoors (depending on the type of bulb), then bring the pots indoors for an extra-early bloom.

❖ Protect flowers and vegetables from early frosts by covering them with sheets of plastic or burlap, or bags, buckets, or bins. Remove the protection when the weather warms up again.

❖ Dig up small annual flowers such as impatiens, and herbs such as basil, sweet marjoram, and chives to keep on your windowsill or in a light garden. They will not grow as well as they do outdoors, but they will be okay for a month or more and will provide garden-fresh flavor and color all the time.

❖ This is your last chance to plant perennial flowers safely. They need several months to develop roots before the soil freezes in winter.

❖ Evergreen trees with needles will lose some now. Don't worry about this natural occurrence, unless needle loss is extreme. In that case, call an arborist to see if there is a problem with the tree.

❖ Enjoy the beautiful fall colors and be certain you have some of the best plants for autumn displays in your yard. Among them are burning bush, maples (especially cultivars such as 'Autumn Flame'), *Enkianthus*, oakleaf hydrangea, sweet gum, red oak, and cut-leaf staghorn sumac.

❖ Plant a witch hazel tree so you can enjoy its spidery yellow flowers, which emerge around now.

LATE OCTOBER

❖ Fertilize deciduous trees and shrubs once the leaves fall but while the roots are still growing. Bury tree spikes or small pockets of a complete granular fertilizer down below turf roots and all around the perimeter of the branch canopy.

❖ Rake up fallen leaves and compost them (see Leaf Composting in this section). Or shred them with a lawn mower and put them on garden beds as a mulch. If you leave piles on the lawn they will make the turf rot.

❖ Look through some of the photos you took of your garden during the summer. Is there one that would make a nice holiday greeting card or a competitive entry in a photo contest? Note the cultivar names on pictured plants for future reference.

❖ Protect evergreen shrubs growing near the house by surrounding them with burlap to support the branches against snow sliding off the roof.

IDEA FOR OCTOBER

Leaf Composting

Since leaves are no longer welcome in landfills, many homeowners are starting their own compost piles. This is a double blessing: it saves landfill space and produces a great soil amendment that is free of weed seeds. The organic matter released when leaves decompose helps aerate and drain our heavy soils. It also holds nutrients and just enough moisture to nourish plant roots. Soils rich in organic matter shelter a community of beneficial microbes that protect against plant disease. Making your own compost also saves you the expense of buying compost, peat moss, or composted cow manure to condition the soil.

If you have only a few leaves, you can chop them up finely with your lawn mower; they will decompose and fertilize the lawn with no further effort on your part. Some lawn mowers are fitted with mulching mechanisms that distribute the chopped leaves evenly over the lawn.

But if leaves fall thickly enough to mat down on the grass, rake and compost them. An easy but less efficient way is to sheet-compost, by layering leaves over a garden bed, then rototilling them in spring. A layer of leaves, however, will keep soil wet much later than ordinary and may not decompose rapidly.

It's better to pile leaves in a long row and chop them with a lawn mower. The smaller the pieces, the faster they will turn into organics. Add some nitrogen fertilizer or compost accelerator (bacteria that break down leaves), then turn the pile once or twice in the winter to provide air to the inside and speed up the decomposition process. To spare your neighbors from sharing the view, you can make your compost pile in a shallow pit in a well-drained area. This will keep leaves warmer so they decompose actively.

(For more on composting, see Making and Using Compost in chapter 6.)

Recipe for October

Quick Pumpkin Muffins

Halve a small pumpkin and scoop out the seeds. Set on a cookie sheet, with the cut sides down, and bake in oven at 350°F for about 30 minutes or until tender. Scoop out the pulp and mash it. Add between 1/2 and 1 cup of the mashed pulp to an instant blueberry muffin mix and prepare according to package directions. You can freeze any excess pumpkin to use at another time. Yield: 4–6 servings.

Notes

NOVEMBER

EARLY NOVEMBER

❖ Plant tender bulbs such as 'Paper White' narcissus for bloom during the holidays. Larger and more expensive amaryllis bulbs may take longer to flower, but their colorful, mammoth blooms are spectacular enough to warrant the wait.

❖ Protect hybrid tea roses for the winter. Remove the overly long canes that would be damaged if they whip around in the wind and cover the graft at the plant's base with a thick layer of leaves and burlap or a styrofoam rose insulator.

❖ Tidy up the garden by edging the beds to give them sharp clean lines.

❖ You can still plant lily bulbs, but give them especially well drained soil because they rot easily.

❖ Notice trees that have interesting bark, a point of beauty you can enjoy all winter. Some of the best include paperbark maple, blood-twigged dogwood, lace-bark pine, and river birches. White birches, though their bark is lovely, are pest-prone.

❖ Resolve next year to plant trees and shrubs with fall and winter fruit that attract birds and brighten up the yard. These include crab apples, viburnum, sumac, fire thorn, cotoneaster, and barberry.

❖ Move all containers of hardy plants into protected locations. If you take them into the garage, water them occasionally. To give evergreens some light, sink them into the soil near your foundation plantings.

LATE NOVEMBER

❖ Make a planter in an interesting basket or heirloom pot or bowl; it will become a conversation piece for the upcoming holidays.

Line the container with plastic so it will not be damaged by the moist soil. Then do something different; plant it with a small red poinsettia and red-leaf rex begonia, or a white poinsettia and silver-leaf aluminum plant and dangling white marbled pothos. Or use gold-dust dracaena with a golden flowered mum and Swedish ivy.

❖ On a warm day, spray an antidesiccant on your rhododendrons to keep the leaves from drying out during winter.

❖ Cut your lawn fairly short so the grass blades won't pack down during winter and encourage fungus diseases to attack.

❖ This is your last opportunity to plant deciduous trees and shrubs. Water them well to help them get established.

IDEA FOR NOVEMBER

The Three Ps for Indoor Gardening Success

Just as the Three *R*s are the foundation of education, three *P*s—pinching, pruning, and potting—are the basis of successful indoor gardening.

• *Pinching* is a simple but important technique used to make annuals or bush-type houseplants grow full and handsome. Nip off the shoot tips on a plant to stimulate side buds to grow into branches.

• *Pruning* involves removal of larger branches and often requires pruning shears or loppers. Prune to remove dead or diseased branches or to encourage resprouting from older, often threadbare, plants. Most indoor trees will require some pruning to prevent them from growing through the roof. Both the shoots and roots can be pruned back by 20 percent every year to maintain a tree at the same size.

• *Potting* is a good task for renewing houseplants. If a plant is pot-bound and its roots slip easily out of the pot or creep out the drainage hole, move it up to a pot an inch or two larger in diameter. Untangle any roots that are tightly matted around the perimeter of the root ball. Replant into fresh soil, using great care not to bury the plant any deeper or set it any shallower than it had been. Firm the fresh soil and water well.

RECIPE FOR NOVEMBER

Golden Autumn Soup
Crisp, early fall apples and tart cider provide good flavor in this squash soup. It may be prepared ahead and reheated.

> 1 1/2 pounds buttercup squash (substitute butternut or acorn)
> 2 tablespoons butter or margarine
> 1 large onion, chopped
> 1 rib celery, chopped
> 3 medium carrots, scraped and diced
> 2 tart apples, peeled, cored and diced
> 3 cups chicken broth
> 1/4 teaspoon grated nutmeg
> 1 teaspoon rubbed sage
> 1/4 teaspoon ground cumin
> 1/4 teaspoon crushed rosemary
> 2 tablespoons butter or margarine (additional)
> 2 tablespoons all-purpose flour
> 1 1/2 cups tart apple cider
> 1/4 teaspoon ground cinnamon
> Garnishes: 1/2 cup grated sharp cheddar cheese, 1/2 cup toasted chopped walnuts.

Cut squash in half, remove seeds. Place squash in a shallow baking pan and bake in preheated 375°F oven until tender, about 40 minutes. Remove from oven and set aside.

In 4-quart Dutch oven or soup pan, melt butter over medium-high heat. Add onions and celery: cook until soft. Remove pulp from squash and place in soup pan. Add carrots, apples, broth, and seasonings. Reduce heat and simmer for 30 minutes. (For a smoother texture, soup may be puréed in food blender or processor.)

In small saucepan, melt additional butter. Whisk in flour and let cook over medium heat for 4 minutes. Gradually whisk in apple cider; add cinnamon. Cook and stir until smooth and slightly thickened. Stir into soup. Taste for seasoning; salt and pepper may be added. Let simmer about 5 minutes.

To serve, ladle soup into bowls and sprinkle with grated cheese and walnuts. Yield: 4–6 servings

(Reprinted with permission from *Cooking With Herb Scents*, edited by Donna Agan, 1991, Western Reserve Herb Society.)

Notes

December

Early December

❖ Prune your evergreen shrubs now to get some fresh greens for holiday decorations. Try this with holly, taxus, rhododendrons, and junipers—but leave pines, spruces, and firs alone.

❖ Spray holiday greens with an antitranspirant (a product that seals plant leaves to reduce moisture loss) and move them outdoors when you are out of the house during the day to keep them fresh longer.

❖ Buy some poinsettias. They come in red, white, pink, yellow, and combinations, and last for months if you keep their soil constantly moist and the plant in reasonably bright light.

❖ Look for pine cones, seedpods, and dried flower heads to use for holiday decorations. Let your imagination run wild for especially creative holiday displays.

❖ Check out the many holiday garden shows around town. (Among the biggest and best are those at The Garden Center of Greater Cleveland and the Rockefeller Park Greenhouse.)

❖ If you are buying a live Christmas tree, dig the hole for it now, before the soil freezes. Move it indoors for as brief a time as possible to give it a better chance of survival outdoors.

❖ Look for Ohio-grown Scotch and white pines, which are fresher than those cut in early fall and shipped in from out of state.

❖ Keep houseplant soil from building up accumulated salts that come in water and fertilizer. Drench the pot and let the extra water run out the bottom to carry salts away. Or when you see a white crust on soil or on the outside of a clay pot, soak the pot—plant and all—for a few minutes to clean away those salts.

Late December

❖ When the soil freezes, cut the boughs off your Christmas tree and use them to mulch perennials that are prone to frost-heaving (shifting out of the ground when the soil freezes and thaws during winter). These include strawberries and coralbells.

❖ If your garden soil is fairly heavy, most other perennials will survive winter best without mulching. Mulch keeps winter soils wetter when they are not frozen and will encourage perennial roots to rot.

❖ Don't salt walks near gardens, especially if all the salt runs off into nearby garden soil or if salt-sensitive rhododendrons are close. Try cat litter or wood ashes instead.

Idea for December

Rise of the Poinsettia

It's hard to imagine a poinsettia dropping its flowers and leaves before New Year's Day. But that's just what they did before Mikkelsen, Inc, an Ashtabula-based plant breeder, developed the first long-lasting cultivars twenty years ago. Now it's not unheard of to have a poinsettia bloom an entire year.

Before 1960 was the era of the primitive poinsettia. Growth retardants, responsible for making today's poinsettia compact, were not available. Growers would mash four-foot-long poinsettia stems until they were flexible. Then to keep the plant bushy, they folded the stem down on itself and secured it with twist ties.

Today, we're used to seeing poinsettias growing in pots. But that's not where they started out sixty years ago, when Paul

Ecke, a California-based pioneer in poinsettias, grew them on his 600-acre ranch. Poinsettias were field-grown, as perennials are today, and each winter Ecke cut the plants back and hilled them up (covered them with soil). In early spring, he dug them with a modified potato digger and shipped them to growers across the country.

Mikkelsen was the first to eliminate the muss and fuss of field-grown plants. He kept a few stock plants alive in his greenhouse during winter. In March he started new stock plants from cuttings. When these rooted and grew, he took more cuttings.

These developments, and extensive breeding programs, have given us long-lasting poinsettias of all sizes and many colors. Poinsettias, like a fine wine, have improved with age.

Recipe for December

Marinated Brussels Sprouts
    A piquant and tasty way to eat your sprouts.

    1 pound Brussels sprouts
    2 tablespoons sweet pickle relish
    2 tablespoons chopped pimiento or red bell pepper
    2 tablespoons finely chopped scallions
    1/4 cup dry white wine
    1 tablespoon vinegar
    1 teaspoon Dijon mustard
    2 tablespoons vegetable oil
    1 clove garlic, finely chopped
    1/2 teaspoon salt
    1/4 teaspoon pepper

Trim and clean Brussels sprouts. Steam or boil them in a small amount of water until tender but firm; drain and cool quickly in ice water to stop the cooking process. In a medium bowl, combine the rest of the ingredients and mix together. Add the drained Brussels sprouts and toss lightly. Cover and refrigerate for at least an hour to let the flavors blend. Serve chilled or at room temperature. Yield: 4 to 6 servings.

(Reprinted with permission from *Recipes from a Kitchen Garden* by Renee Shepherd, 1990, Shepherd's Garden Publishing, Felton, CA.)

NOTES

WHERE TO LOOK
FOR CURRENT GARDENING REMINDERS

Newspapers
- *The Plain Dealer* (Wednesday Food section; Friday; Saturday Real Estate magazine; Sunday)
- *Sun Newspapers* (Thursday)
- *Akron Beacon Journal* (Wednesday)
- *Elyria Chronicle Telegram* (Friday)
- *Lake County News-Herald* (Friday)
- *Lorain Journal* (Friday)

Magazines/Newsletters
- *Garden Center Bulletin*, The Garden Center of Greater Cleveland
- *Ohio Gardening*, Cuyahoga County Cooperative Extension Service

Other Media
- Northcoast Gardener, Alan Hirt's 8–10 a.m. Sunday radio show on WWWE.
- Compuserve Garden Forum. A library of monthly garden ideas and a network of other gardeners are available on this on-line service, which you can join if you own a computer and modem. (For information on joining, call Compuserve at 800-848-8990.)